Prayers for One Another

Prayers for One Another

Forward Movement
Cincinnati, Ohio

ISBN: 978-0-88028-536-0
Printed in China

Forward Movement
inspire disciples. empower evangelists.

Contents

Foreword

Here at Forward Movement, we regularly pause in our work to meet for prayer. We pray, certainly, for our individual and collective needs. But mostly we share intentions of prayer that reach beyond our own circle:

> We pray for friends and family, both near and far.
>
> We pray for our enemies.
>
> We pray with the news: for those affected by disasters in the headlines.
>
> We pray for our readers: in parishes, in prisons, deployed overseas, right around the corner.
>
> We pray for anyone who's sent in a prayer request online.
>
> We pray for you.

From our own collective life of prayer, here at Forward Movement, in the Episcopal Church, we offer now this collection of *Prayers for One Another.* Our hope is that this book will help you to pray for others, earnestly bringing their needs before God.

Will our prayer help those for whom we pray? We believe by God's grace that it does.

Certainly, we know that our prayer changes us. Praying for others teaches us how to love them, widening our hearts—prayer by prayer—opening us beyond ourselves. Praying for others teaches us, perhaps, to love a little more as God does: encompassing all the world in a vast embrace of love.

The core of this volume is a collection of intercessory prayers, grouped by theme. Many of these prayers may be familiar to you: drawn from the Book of Common Prayer, from other resources in Forward Movement's nearly hundred-year history, as well as from the vast stores of our Christian tradition. Most of these intercessions follow the form of the collect, the prayer form that is at the heart of the Anglican and Episcopal corporate prayer tradition. This through-line is no accident. When we pray such familiar words, grouped in familiar patterns, we join with the company of all those in heaven and on earth who share in praying them with us, across time and in God's eternity. We hope that this collection of intercessory collects will help you to join your voice in prayer with all God's people and for all God's people.

Like its predecessors, *Prayers New and Old* and *Prayers for All Occasions,* this book seeks to broaden the scope of our answers to the question "for whom and for what shall we pray?" We seek to be broad but, of course, cannot be exhaustive in these prayers. One slim volume can't hope to contain a prayer for every person, group, or concern that needs our intercession. But we hope that the groups named here might open your heart to those other concerns toward which God is drawing your attention. We also propose a plan for intercession across the week, intended to help those who wish to plan their private devotions more systematically.

In the second half of the volume, we've included a wide selection of other prayers, diverse in form and theme: prayers of praise and thanksgiving, daily devotions, prayers for families, prayers for individual needs, litanies, and blessings.

Many of these prayers, we hope, will be new to you: borrowed from sister churches or written particularly for this volume by friends around the world. In this volume of prayers for one another, we want to glimpse how one another pray around our church. The voices of those we call "saints" sit here alongside words written by those in the pews today, reminding us that, when we pray, we are knit together with the whole company of God's faithful, in heaven and on earth. Remember that even as we pray for one another, *they* pray for *us*.

The prayers you'll find in this book are, in many ways, an eclectic, personal assortment. This beautiful hodge-podge has made its way here because these prayers have a special place in the praying hearts of the people who, across more than a decade, have brought this collection together. They are some of our beloved prayers. We hope they might become yours, too.

However you use this book, we hope that it will bless your praying life and invite you to bring the diverse needs of yourself, our world, and one another to God.

We pray above all that it brings you nearer to those you love—to those you don't—and deeper into the heart of the God who loves us all.

Intercessions

God give grace to the living, and to the departed rest; and forgiveness to the Church, and to the nations peace and concord; and to us sinners life in the glory of His presence. Amen.

Weekly Plan for Intercessions

These intercessions are collected into sections to help you to pray around the world and across the week, reaching from your nearest orbit to the furthest reaches of the globe.

SUNDAY | For the Parish
Prayers for our local parishes, clergy, lay leaders, and all who minister

MONDAY | For Home
Prayers for our homes, families and relations, and those who are dear to us

TUESDAY | For Our Community
Prayers for our towns and cities, and for all who live and work in them

WEDNESDAY | For Our Country
Prayers for our country, its leaders and government, and all who serve the common good

THURSDAY | For the World
Prayers for all nations and peoples of the world, for those living in conflict and those working toward peace, and for the whole creation

FRIDAY | For the Church Universal
Prayers for the Church worldwide,
for all Christians, and for the coming of the Kingdom

SATURDAY | For the Sick & Suffering
Prayers for all who sorrow, in our own lives and around the world

For the Parish

Prayers for our local parishes,
clergy, lay leaders,
and all who minister

For the Parish

O God, you have brought us into the fellowship of your dear Son: Lead us all in this church ever closer day by day to you and to one another, that we may become of one heart and mind in love toward you; and grant that our common life and work in sacrificial service may help to extend your kingdom here and in all the world. *Amen.*

✠

Almighty and everlasting God, you govern all things in heaven and on earth; Grant to this parish and congregation all things we need. Strengthen the faithful, arouse the indifferent; visit and relieve the sick; bless and protect the children; restore the penitent; and bring us all to be of one heart and mind, to the honor of your Name. *Amen.*

✠

O God, make the door of this house wide enough to receive all who need your fellowship and ours, and narrow enough to shut out all envy, pride, and strife. Make its threshold smooth enough to be no stumbling-block to children nor to straying feet, but rugged and strong enough to turn back the tempter's power. God, make the door of this house the gateway to your eternal kingdom. *Amen.*

✠

Almighty and Everlasting God, hear our prayers and grant to this parish all things necessary for its spiritual well-being: enlighten and guide our leaders, our clergy, wardens, and vestry; strengthen and increase the faithful, visit and relieve the sick, turn and renew the hard-hearted or careless, bring again those who have wandered; remove from us anything that resists your grace or hinders your purposes; make all of us one united voice to sing your praise and to give witness to your goodness; through Jesus Christ our Lord. *Amen.*

For Youth in the Parish

Tender God, we entrust to your loving care the children and young people of our parish. Bless their questioning and their exploration. Call forth their gifts, consecrate their joys, and soothe their sorrows. Keep these young people safe, O God, and help them to grow in their knowledge and love of you and of your Church—that wonderful and sometimes confusing mystery. In all things, make them know that they are never alone and that you are with them always; through Jesus Christ our Lord. *Amen.*

– Cody Maynus, Diocese of Minnesota

For Those Seeking Baptism

O God, you prepared your disciples for the coming of the Spirit through the teaching of your Son Jesus Christ: Make the hearts and minds of your servants ready to receive the blessing of the Holy Spirit, that they may be filled with the strength of his presence; through Jesus Christ our Lord. *Amen.*

For All the Baptized

God of faithfulness, in every age you call women and men to make known your love: May we be so strengthened in the ministries of love and reconciliation to which we are called by virtue of our baptism, that we may always witness to your holy Name. *Amen.*

For Volunteers

Almighty and everlasting God, by whose Spirit the whole body of your faithful people is governed and sanctified: Receive our supplications and prayers, which we offer before you for all members of your holy Church, that in their vocation and ministry they may truly and devoutly serve you; through our Lord and Savior Jesus Christ, who lives and reigns with you, in the unity of the Holy Spirit, one God, now and for ever. *Amen.*

For Altar Guilds

Risen Jesus, at the cross your disciples
washed your body
and dressed you in fair linen,
and you revealed yourself to the women
who came to care for your body early in
the morning:
Teach me the same faithfulness and
tenderness
as I care for the vessels and linens
that will carry your risen Body and
healing Blood.

Grant that I may join your beloved disciples
and find you not dead but alive;
not absent but calling to me by name.
Banish my anxiety and fill me with peace
as I lead others into your presence;
for the sake of your love. *Amen.*

– Noah Stansbury, Diocese of Texas

For Church Choirs

O God, who inspired David the King both to write songs and to appoint singers for your worship: Give grace to the singers in your Church, that with psalms, and hymns, and spiritual songs, we may sing and make music to the glory of your Name; through Jesus Christ our Lord. *Amen.*

For the Vestry

Lord, we ask you to craft our vestry into a vessel: strong in faith, faithful in purpose, purposeful in mission. Build the vestry members into leaders in your church, here in this parish and beyond. Fill their hearts with your Spirit, that they may never tire of seeking you and helping bring your kingdom to fulfillment. We ask all this in the name of the one who walked upon the water, leading his disciples in miracle after miracle behind him, Jesus Christ our Lord. *Amen.*

For Lay Ministers

O God, you have reconciled the world to yourself through Christ, and entrusted to all the ministry of reconciliation. Bless all your people whom you have called to lay ministry. Strengthen them for your work in this world, according to the gifts they have been given. Grant them courage and joy to bear witness to Christ wherever they may be, that the light of your love may shine brightly throughout the world. *Amen.*

For Disciples

Heavenly Father, may we learn more and more to live each day under your direction and guidance, according to your will, knowing that you will not fail to provide vision, understanding, strength, wisdom, and courage to those who are open to receive them. *Amen.*

For Deacons

Lord Jesus, who came among us as one who serves, grant to your deacon, *N.*, patience and faithfulness that by *his* work, the Church may come to understand better the needs of the world and by *his* proclamation of the Gospel, we may hear your call to serve as you have served us and in words and action, proclaim the Good News. *Amen.*

For a Priest

O Lord Jesus Christ, good shepherd of your people and our great high priest standing before God on our behalf, pour out your blessing on *N.*, that *she* may serve you as a faithful steward of the sacraments of grace, an effective witness to the Gospel and as a conscientious pastor to this parish *(or for...)*, that your Church may be strengthened and equipped for its mission; through the same Jesus Christ our Lord. *Amen.*

For the Bishop

Grant to our Bishop, *N.* gracious Lord, wisdom and understanding to know your will for the Church, a heart that knows and cares for our people in their parishes and missions, and such clarity of expression, patience in teaching, and courage in leadership that this diocese may stand secure in its faith and constant in its service to the world for the sake of Christ. *Amen.*

For Visitors

Lord, you stand at the door and knock: prepare us to open it. Lord, you come as child; as stranger; as teacher and friend: prepare us to welcome you. Lord, you come as joy; as disturbance; as surprise: prepare us to receive you as you are. Lord, you are in the face of every guest: help us to reveal your face as well. May there be no outsiders here; no peripheries; no falseness or fear, but only a love which draws all things to its center. *Amen.*

For Those Seeking a Church Home

God who lit the way for your people in exile: Guide your children who are now seeking their next church home. Lead them to a place where they will be welcomed; where their gifts will be put to use; where they can take their place as members of the Body of your Son. Strengthen them for the journey, and grant them a sense of your nearness even as they wait, until they find their way home to your church in this life, and to the fullness of your presence in the life to come. *Amen.*

For New Members

Heavenly Father, thank you for guiding new members into our parish family. We are elated that they have chosen to serve as the hands and feet of your Son Jesus in this small part of your kingdom on earth. As we embrace these new parishioners with loving arms, we pray for wisdom to ensure that genuine connections are made, that all feel welcome and able to transition easily into the life of the church. Guided by the Holy Spirit, may they share their time, talent, and treasure with the congregation in a meaningful way, to your honor and glory. May reciprocal growth and maturity flourish among all of us. Forever your humble servants, we ask this prayer in the blessed name of your Son, our Savior, Jesus Christ, *Amen.*

– Karen J. Vaughn, Diocese of Pennsylvania

For Those Calling a New Priest

Almighty God, we pray for the guidance of your Holy Spirit as we seek a new priest for our church. You know our special needs and the task that lies to our hand. Direct us in our search and give us insight to perceive the leader you would choose for us. And we further pray, O Lord, that in this time of waiting we may all devote ourselves afresh to your service, so that nothing be lost of the faithful work of the past. *Amen.*

For New Ministry Together

Beloved Guide,
As we embark on this new adventure:
For a willingness to learn, we ask that you open our minds;
For grounding in your wisdom, we ask that you open our hearts;
For a sense of delight, we ask that you open our curiosity.
We ask to become listeners to one another, in order to find a common sense of direction.
We ask to become listeners to you, in order to find the path forward.
Thank you for all that we are together.
May we be instruments of life-giving love, grace, and mercy.
Amen.

– Marna Franson, Diocese of Northern Michigan

For Church Growth

Almighty God, you call your church to witness that in Christ we are reconciled to you: Help us so to proclaim the good news of your love, that all who hear it may turn to you. *Amen.*

For Churches Closing

Lord God, in your great goodness you have blessed the ministries of *N.* over the years: Receive our praise and thanksgiving for the blessings, help, and comfort which you bestowed upon your people in this place. We pray that just as you have blessed your community of *N.*, you will bless its members in their ministries going forward, wherever that may be. Comfort them by the knowledge that your presence is not tied to any place or building, but can be found wherever two or three gather in your Name. *Amen.*

For Our Neighbors

Source of love,
we pray for our neighbors:
those we know well
and those we pass without speaking.

Help us be good neighbors:
attentive without intrusion,
generous without expectation,
present without judgment.

Open our eyes to the needs around us
and our hearts to respond with compassion.
May our shared spaces be shaped
by respect and mutual concern.

Let our presence reflect
your love made visible
in ordinary ways.
May we love. Always.
Amen.

– *Melissa Rau, Diocese of Southwest Florida*

For the Diocese

O God, by your grace you have called us in this Diocese to a goodly fellowship of faith. Bless our Bishops(s) *N.* [and *N.*], and other clergy, and all our people. Grant that your Word may be truly preached and truly heard, your Sacraments faithfully administered and faithfully received. By your Spirit, fashion our lives according to the example of your Son, and grant that we may show the power of your love to all among whom we live; through Jesus Christ our Lord. *Amen.*

For Home

Prayers for our homes,
families and relations,
and those who are dear to us

For Our Homes

Almighty God, our heavenly Father, you set the solitary in families: We commend to your continual care the homes in which your people dwell. Put far from them, we pray, every root of bitterness, the desire of vainglory, and the pride of life. Fill them with faith, virtue, knowledge, temperance, patience, godliness. Knit together in constant affection those who, in holy wedlock, have been made one flesh. Turn the hearts of the parents to the children, and the hearts of children to the parents; and so enkindle fervent charity among us all, that we may evermore be kindly affectioned one to another. *Amen.*

For Fellowship

O God, who hast bound us together in this bundle of life, give us grace to understand how our lives depend upon the courage, the industry, the honesty, and the integrity of our fellow humans; that we may be faithful in our responsibilities to them; through Jesus Christ our Lord. *Amen.* – *Reinhold Niebuhr (1892–1971)*

For Families

Heavenly Father, we thank you for your mercies which are new every morning: For health and strength, for this day with its fresh opportunities for work and service. Bless each one of us, and hold us together in your love and in love of you. We pray for your help and guidance as we face the duties to be done, the decisions to be made, the temptations that may beset us, the disappointments that may await us. Guide us, strengthen us, keep us; and grand that in all things we may act worthily of our Christian calling. *Amen.*

For Those Who Depend On Us

You know our hearts, Lord, that all you have given us, we intend to spend on those who depend on us, and to use it all in their service and yours. O Lord God, keep watch over those who depend on us day and night. Tenderly spread your wings to protect them, stretch forth your right hand to bless them. Pour into their hearts your Holy Spirit to abide with them, to refresh them, to give them hope, to make them humble before you, and to kindle in them the fire of your Love. May the Holy Spirit, the comforter, protect them in temptation and be their strength in all the trials and tribulations of this life. *Amen.*

For Married Couples

Almighty God, giver of life and love, bless *N.* and *N.* Grant them wisdom and devotion in the ordering of their common life, that each may be to the other a strength in need, a counselor in perplexity, a comfort in sorrow, and a companion in joy. And so knit their wills together in your will and their spirits in your Spirit, that they may live together in love and peace all the days of their life; through Jesus Christ our Lord. *Amen.*

For Those Whose Marriage Has Ended

God of compassion and grace, in your steadfast love accompany *NN*. As you ever work to restore and renew your people, overcome bitterness with your joy, hatred with your love, brokenness with your life; and give us hope through the death and resurrection of your Son, Jesus Christ our Lord. *Amen.*

For All Who Care for Children

Heavenly Father, from whose care we learn our pattern of parenthood, give to those who have the care of children the spirit of wisdom, patience, and love, so that the house in which they grow up may be to them an image of your kingdom, and the care of their parents a likeness of your love. *Amen.*

For Parents

O Gracious God, we commend our children to you; let them know you to be their God and protector, their creator and savior, the rock of their life and the goal toward which they move. Pour your grace into their hearts, and confirm and multiply in them the gifts of the Holy Spirit, that they may abound daily in grace and in the knowledge of Jesus; may they find joy and wonder in all your works, and grow in faith, hope, and love toward you and all people. Of your infinite goodness, provide whatever they lack from our frailty or negligence. As you have called us to this great work, awaken in us the patience, the wisdom, and the love necessary to complete it, that your presence may be the joy of our home and our eternal hope. *Amen.*

For Mothers

Mother God, who birthed the universe and us in it,

Bless all who fill the role of mother.

We thank you for those who have given birth to us physically or spiritually or emotionally.

We thank you for the mothers who have reared us, shaped us, nurtured us, held us close, and let us go.

We pray for mothers whom we mourn because of death or brokenness or alienation.

We pray for mothers and would-be mothers who mourn the loss of children or the inability to bear children, and the hard choices they have had to make.

We ask for your healing in our imperfect lives.

Be with us this day, loving God who entered our human life through a mother, and bless all who strive to embrace your way of life. *Amen.*

– Barbara Ballenger, Diocese of Pennsylvania

For Those Awaiting Childbirth

Lord Jesus Christ, whose blessed Mother knew the joy of anticipation as well as the fears of childbirth: Grant your servant *N.* the grace of a quiet mind during these days of waiting, and the strength and courage that *she* shall need when the time of delivery is near. And may the child that shall be born bring blessing, and be a blessing always. *Amen.*

For Those Who Have Recently Given Birth

O gracious God, we give you humble and hearty thanks that you have preserved through the pain and anxiety of childbirth your servant *N.*, who desires now to offer you her praises and thanksgivings. Grant, most merciful Father, that by your help she may live faithfully according to your will in this life, and finally partake of everlasting glory in the life to come; through Jesus Christ our Lord. *Amen.*

For New Parents

Lord, wrap in your tender care all new parents struggling with the gifts so long awaited: weighted with sleepless nights, heavy hopes, and tender fears. Open their hearts to the blessings of this time. Grant them energy, hope, and company, in Jesus' name. *Amen.*

For Those Struggling to Conceive

God our creator, who birthed the cosmos and fills everything with breath, sustain *N.* with your life-giving spirit, even now, in this time of trial. You know they long for a child; you count the hairs of their heads and note the fall of each sparrow: please soften the ache of their current disappointments; strengthen their hope; and give them patience to trust in your timeline and your providence. Be with them and help them to be with each other, as they mourn lost hopes and hope anew. We ask this in the name of the babe, born in Bethlehem, and given for all your children, Jesus Christ our Lord. *Amen.*

For Fathers

Father God, who provides for us with wisdom and grace, bless all who fill the role of father.

We thank you for all those who have parented us physically, spiritually, or emotionally.

Thank you for the fathers who have reared us, nurtured us, guided, held us close, and let us go. We pray for the fathers whom we mourn because of death, brokenness, or alienation.

We pray for fathers and would-be fathers who grieve the loss of children or the inability to have children.

Be with us this day, loving God, Father to your son, Jesus Christ, and through your Holy Spirit bless all who strive to embrace your way of love.

Amen.

– Barbara Ballenger, Diocese of Pennsylvania

For Children

O Lord Jesus Christ, you took children into your arms and blessed them. We pray you to keep our children ever enfolded by your love. Help them to grow in love of you; save them from evil; strengthen them against the impulse of self-will; inspire in them a high sense of truth and of the duty of human service; and give them grace to follow day by day in the steps of your most holy life. *Amen.*

✠

O God, you have taught us through your blessed Son that whoever receives a little child in the name of Christ receives Christ himself: We give you thanks for the blessing you have bestowed upon this family in giving them a child. Confirm their joy by a lively sense of your presence with them, and give them calm strength and patient wisdom as they seek to bring this child to love all that is true and noble, just and pure, lovable and gracious, excellent and admirable, following the example of our Lord and Savior, Jesus Christ. *Amen.*

O Lord Jesus Christ, you embrace children with the arms of your mercy, and make them living members of your Church; Give them grace, we pray, to stand fast in your faith, to obey your word, and to abide in your love; that being made strong by your Holy Spirit they may resist temptation and overcome evil; and may rejoice in the life that now is, and dwell with you in the life that is to come. *Amen.*

Lord, as once the mothers of Judea brought their children to you that you might bless them, so now we come to you, bringing with us in our hearts those children dear to us. We humbly entrust them to your never failing mercy and almighty love, asking only that they may do your will throughout their lives, and that you will keep them close to you for ever. *Amen.*

For Those Who Have Lost a Child

Grant that those who grieve may have faith to entrust this child to your keeping and meet the sorrows of the days to come with patience and hope; for we know that nothing, not death nor life, nor sorrow nor pain, will separate us from your love, and it is in your Name we pray. *Amen.*

For the Young

Lord God of our ancestors, we thank you for what you have done and will continue to do with our daughters and sons. Walk with them in life, and keep the evil one from obstructing their path. You see all; you know where the water is deep. Keep them from danger. Order their steps and guide their feet while they run the race of faith. May the good work that you have begun in them be brought to completion at the day of Jesus Christ, in whose name we pray. *Amen.*

For Young Adults

O Giver of Life, who delights in doing a new thing: Look with compassion upon young people who are stepping into new and greater independence. Grant them joy in their newfound agency and wisdom in their use of it. Bring them safe and joy-filled communities, friends, and mentors. As they separate from what is familiar, where there has been pain, let distance bring healing; where there has been comfort, let distance bring growth. Guide them in the discovery of their gifts and how best to serve others, and open their hands to graciously release what it is time to leave behind. In all things let this new life bring them closer to you, who holds us in all times, now and forever. *Amen.*

– Noah Stansbury, Diocese of Texas

For the Aged

Look with mercy, O God our Father, on all whose increasing years bring them weakness, distress, or isolation. Provide for them homes of dignity and peace; give them understanding helpers, and the willingness to accept help; and, as their strength diminishes, increase their faith and their assurance of your love. This we ask in the name of Jesus Christ our Lord. *Amen.*

For Pets

Creator of all life, we ask your blessing on all those beings who share with us this world you've made: both those beyond our windows and those within our walls. You note the fall of a sparrow and so you know how precious in our sight are our animal companions. May they know safety and joy, fulfillment and connection; may we bless their lives daily as they bless ours. Thank you for entrusting them to our care; we entrust them—and our whole lives—to yours; in the name of Jesus. *Amen.*

For Loved Ones Far Away

Almighty God, we entrust all who are dear to us to thy never-failing care and love, for this life and the life to come, knowing that thou art doing for them better things than we can desire or pray for; through Jesus Christ our Lord. *Amen.*

For Estranged Families

Lord Jesus, who left eternity behind to be born into a human family, with all its realities and flaws, we offer to your loving care all families who are fractured or hurting. When it is right to find reconciliation, open the hearts that have closed; soften resentments; kindle the desire for return. And when reconciliation would be harmful or wrong, we ask you to create separate paths of healing. Help us to remember that we are all siblings in one family, O Prince of Peace. *Amen.*

For Those with Whom We Disagree

God who moves over the waters, you call your people across borders and barriers to be baptized into the death and resurrection of your Son: Hear our prayer for those brothers and sisters with whom we disagree. Where our hearts are hardened against others, give us hearts of mercy and kindness. Where others challenge your love and mercy, grant us the strength to stand firm in the truth of your love. Make us part of your new creation, where everyone will be reconciled to you. *Amen.*

For Those Who Live Alone

Almighty God, whose son had nowhere to lay his head: Grant that those who live alone may not be lonely in their solitude, but that, following in his steps, they may find fulfillment in loving you and their neighbors; through Jesus Christ our Lord. *Amen.*

For the Lonely

Lord Jesus, in Gethsemane, your friends were not able to stay awake and watch with you, and, when you were taken, they all fled leaving you alone; remember with compassion and for good those who are alone; those who have lost friends or family to death; those whose lives have been solitary because of work or particular burdens. We pray also for those who in selfishness or other faults have broken every tie, those whose guilt or sin leaves them alone or despised. We pray for those who have been falsely accused and shunned for no reasons, those embittered through what they have endured, and for all caught in the isolation of mental confusion.

In all of these, O Lord, let your Spirit work forgiveness and reconciliation, renewal and hope; give to each of us such a sense of your abiding love, such a confidence in the communion of saints and such a heart that as we turn toward you, we turn also toward each other, in perfect charity and in the bonds of friendship; for you have called us friends and welcome us all into the one and eternal kingdom. *Amen.*

For the Joyful

O Lord, you have warned us that you will require much of those to whom much is given: Grant that we, who have received much, may strive together, by our prayers, hard work, and gifts, to extend to those who know you not what we so richly enjoy. *Amen.*

For Families in Times of Transition

Grant us, Lord, not to be anxious about earthly things, but to love things heavenly; and even now, while we are placed among things that are passing away, to hold fast to those that shall endure; through Jesus Christ our Lord, who lives and reigns with you and the Holy Spirit, one God, for ever and ever. *Amen.*

For Families in Turmoil

Almighty God, you alone can bring into order the unruly wills and affections of sinners: Grant your people grace to love what you command and desire what you promise; that, among the swift and varied changes of the world, our hearts may surely there be fixed where true joys are to be found; through Jesus Christ our Lord, who lives and reigns with you and the Holy Spirit, one God, now and for ever. *Amen.*

For Our Departed Loved Ones

Father of all, we pray to you for all those whom we love but see no longer. Grant them your peace; let light perpetual shine upon them; and in your loving wisdom and almighty power, work in them the good purpose of your perfect will; through Jesus Christ our Lord. *Amen.*

For Our Community

Prayers for our towns and cities,
and for all who live and work in them

For the Neighborhood

God our creator, by your holy prophet Jeremiah you taught your ancient people to seek the welfare of the cities in which they lived. We commend our neighborhood to your care, that it might be kept free from social strife and decay. Give us strength of purpose and concern for others, that we may create here a community of justice and peace where your will may be done; through your Son, Jesus Christ our Lord. *Amen.*

For All Who Work

Almighty God our heavenly Father, you declare your glory and show forth your handiwork in the heavens and in the earth: Deliver us in our various occupations from the service of self alone, that we may do the work you give us to do in truth and beauty and for the common good; for the sake of him who came among us as one who serves, your Son Jesus Christ our Lord, who lives and reigns with you and the Holy Spirit, one God, for ever and ever. *Amen.*

For Laborers

God of daily bread, we pray for all who labor: for work that is seen and work that goes unnoticed. Bless those who work the land, those who prepare and serve food, and those whose bodies grow tired so that others may be nourished. Grant dignity to their work and fairness to their wages. Give them strength for the day and rest that truly restores. May we never take for granted the labor that sustains our lives, and may justice accompany gratitude. *Amen.*

For Those Who Labor for Our Food

Blessed are you, Lord God King of the universe, who creates varieties of nourishment. May we be mindful of the many who work for the food we eat. We give thanks for all who have been part of the community who worked to bring this meal for our nourishment, especially those we name either silently or aloud. Nourish our bodies with this food, our souls with the connections to those who grew and prepared it in any way, and our lives with the faith that fills us. *Amen.*

For Those in Active Professions

O God, Father of us all, we pray for those who toil in mill or mine, for those by whose labor we are clothed and fed, for those who work in the darkness of the earth, for those who build and adorn our houses, for those who trade in shop or market, and for those who travel by land, sea, and air. May our service and our merchandise be holy unto the Lord. May we do justly and love mercy and walk humbly with you. *Amen.*

For Public Safety Workers

Magnificent Father God, we give thanks for those who work in public safety occupations and lift them up in prayer. Please imbue them with strength, patience, courage, and the ability to discern the humanity of every person they encounter. With your help, may these public servants discharge their duties faithfully, respectfully, and honorably, always keeping top of mind their responsibility to protect and serve the public. Please cover them with your hedge of protection throughout the day, to keep them safe from all hurt, harm, and danger. May your call to us—to act justly, to love mercy and to walk humbly with our God—resonate in their hearts each day. We ask this prayer in the name of your son, our Savior, Jesus Christ, *Amen.*

– Karen J. Vaughn, Diocese of Pennsylvania

For Healthcare Professionals

Sanctify, O Lord, those whom you have called to the study and practice of the arts of healing, and to the prevention of disease and pain. Strengthen them by your life-giving Spirit, that by their ministries the health of the community may be promoted and your creation glorified; through Jesus Christ our Lord. *Amen.*

For Caregivers

Jesus, born of Mary, you came among us as one who serves: Bless *N.* and all who spend their days in care for others. Let their work be eased by the knowledge of your own loving care. Grant them glimpses of your presence in both the tedious and joyous moments of this day. Strengthen them for their work and grant them peace and rest along the way. *Amen.*

For Educators and Students

Almighty God, the fountain of all wisdom: Enlighten by your Holy Spirit those who teach and those who learn, that, rejoicing in the knowledge of your truth, they may worship you and serve you from generation to generation; through Jesus Christ our Lord, who lives and reigns with you and the Holy Spirit, one God, for ever and ever. *Amen.*

For Travelers

O God, our heavenly Father, whose glory fills the whole creation, and whose presence we find wherever we go: Preserve those who travel [in particular *N.*]; surround them with your loving care; protect them from every danger; and bring them in safety to their journey's end; through Jesus Christ our Lord. *Amen.*

For Volunteers

Generous God, who with humility took on human form and assumed a posture of loving service, bless your willing servants as they offer themselves to our neighbors; bless their hands to do meaningful work, their minds to be transformed by new experiences, their words to bring encouragement and foster true community, that in their presence your goodness will be made known, by your abiding Spirit. *Amen.*

– Caroline Hamilton-Arnold
Disciples of Christ, Houston, TX

For the Unemployed

Heavenly Father, we remember before you those who suffer want and anxiety from lack of work. Guide the people of this land so to use our public and private wealth that all may find suitable and fulfilling employment, and receive just payment for their labor; through Jesus Christ our Lord. *Amen.*

For Good Will

Take from us, O Lord, all bitterness and hatred. Keep our hearts in confident trust. Make us reverent in the use of our freedom and deepen within us the roots of faith and righteousness. Give to us the spirit of good will so that, when the day of conflict ends, the barriers of race may be broken, and we may enter into the enjoyment of a nobler service for God and for all peoples. Through Jesus Christ our Lord. *Amen.*

For the LGBTQ+ Community

God of all creation, you have made us in your image, a rainbow of every color, culture, gender expression, language, orientation, and nation; grant that, when we look at one another, we may see you, expressed in yet another language of love; and grant that we may honor your holy presence in every life. We pray because of Jesus, who shows us the way. *Amen.*

– Kay Sylvester, Diocese of Los Angeles

For Trans & Nonbinary People

God in the beginning you created day and night and sunrises. You created the water and the land and the shoreline that is ever changing. In these places of in-between, of both and of neither, you created beauty, diversity, and life. We name and celebrate that you created our nonbinary siblings, reminding us that in your creation there is an infinite and glorious diversity to discover, declare, and embrace. *Amen.*

– Ruth Marston-Bihl
United Methodist Church, Seattle, WA

For Outcasts

Lord Jesus, who befriended the vulnerable and loved outcasts. Strengthen those who walk in your way to be outspoken in love and radical in acceptance of all people, that we may love as you love. We ask this in the name of the loving God, liberating Son, and life-giving Spirit. *Amen.*

For All God's Beloved

Holy God,
you who knit us together in Love,
you call and claim us wonderful.
You remind us that every body you form
shines with your divine image.

Search us and know us, O God.
Surround our trans and nonbinary siblings
with the fierce tenderness of your love.
Let no lie or hatred drown out the truth
that they are your beloved,
crafted with dignity and delight.

Unmake our prejudice,
deepen our compassion,
and shape us into people who honor
the belovedness
you have woven into us all. *Amen.*

– Deon Johnson, Diocese of Missouri

For God's Messengers

Send us, O God, as thy messengers, to hearts without a home, to lives without love, to the crowds without a compass. Send us to the children whom none have blessed, to the famished whom none have fed, to the sick whom none have visited, to the fallen whom none have lifted, to the leper whom none have touched, to the bereaved whom none have comforted. Kindle thy flame on the altars of our hearts, that others may be warmed thereby; cause thy light to shine in our souls, that others may see the way; keep our sympathies and insight ready, our wills keen, our hands quick to help our brothers in their need; for Christ's sake. *Amen.*

For Our Country

Prayers for our country,
its leaders and government,
and all who serve the common good

For Citizens

O God, teach us your people to rely on your strength and to accept our responsibilities to our fellow citizens. May we elect trustworthy leaders so that the rights of all may be protected and our nation be enabled to fulfill your purposes. *Amen.*

For Servants of the Common Good

Grant, O God, that your holy and life-giving Spirit may so move every human heart [and especially the hearts of the people of this land], that barriers which divide us may crumble, suspicions disappear, and hatreds cease; that our divisions being healed, we may live in justice and peace; through Jesus Christ our Lord. *Amen.*

For Leaders

Heavenly Father, whose blessed Son came not to be served but to serve: Bless all who, following in his steps, give themselves to the service of others; that with wisdom, patience, and courage, they may minister in his Name to the suffering, the friendless, and the needy; for the love of him who laid down his life for us, your Son our Savior Jesus Christ. *Amen.*

For the President of the United States and All in Civil Authority

O Lord our Governor, whose glory is in all the world: We commend this nation to thy merciful care, that, being guided by thy Providence, we may dwell secure in thy peace. Grant to the President of the United States, the Governor of this State (*or* Commonwealth), and to all in authority, wisdom and strength to know and to do thy will. Fill them with the love of truth and righteousness, and make them ever mindful of their calling to serve this people in thy fear; through Jesus Christ our Lord, who liveth and reigneth with thee and the Holy Spirit, one God, world without end. *Amen.*

For Congress and Legislatures

O God, the fountain of wisdom, whose will is good and gracious, and whose law is truth: We beseech you so to guide and bless our Senators and Representatives in Congress assembled (*or* in the Legislature of this State, *or* Commonwealth), that they may enact such laws as shall please you, to the glory of your Name and the welfare of this people; through Jesus Christ our Lord. *Amen.*

For Courts of Justice

Almighty God, who sits in the throne judging right: We humbly beseech you to bless the courts of justice and the magistrates in all this land; and give to them the spirit of wisdom and understanding, that they may discern the truth, and impartially administer the law in the fear of you alone; through him who shall come to be our Judge, your Son our Savior Jesus Christ. *Amen.*

For All Who Seek Justice

O God, you have bound us together in a common life. Help us, in the midst of our struggles for justice and truth, to confront one another without hatred or bitterness, and to work together with mutual forbearance and respect; through Jesus Christ our Lord. *Amen.*

For Neighbors in Need

O Lord, we pray that you will hasten the time when no one shall live in contentment while a neighbor has need. Inspire in us and in all people the consciousness that we are not our own but yours and our neighbors', for his sake who prayed that we might all be one in him, Christ Jesus our Lord. *Amen.*

For Sound Government

O Lord our Governor, bless the leaders of our national, state, and local governments, that we may be a people at peace among ourselves and a blessing to other nations of the earth. *Amen.*

For Voters in Times of Election

Governor of the cosmos, watch over our engagement in the dual citizenship of your reign and this earthly nation. Help us choose wisely those who will govern for the good and just use of our resources. Remind us that our freedom comes with responsibility to you and others. *Amen.*

– Andy Doyle, Diocese of Texas

For Immigrants and Exiles

Dear Lord, our Father, you have made of one blood all the nations upon the earth and called all people your children: Bless all immigrants and exiles, and especially those who have come to this land. May their coming be a blessing to the nation and to them. Help us to labor together with them in fellowship to build here a righteous society founded on brotherhood and justice. We ask all in the Name of him through whom your kingdom comes. *Amen.*

For All Who Share This Nation

Almighty God, giver of all good things:

We thank you for the natural majesty and beauty of this land. They restore us, though we often destroy them.
Heal us.

We thank you for the great resources of this nation. They make us rich, though we often exploit them.
Forgive us.

We thank you for the men and women who have made this country strong. They are models for us, though we often fall short of them.
Inspire us.

We thank you for the torch of liberty which has been lit in this land. It has drawn people from every nation, though we have often hidden from its light.
Enlighten us.

We thank you for the faith we have inherited in all its rich variety. It sustains our life, though we have been faithless again and again.
Renew us.

Help us, O Lord, to finish the good work here begun. Strengthen our efforts to blot out ignorance and prejudice, and to abolish poverty and crime. And hasten the day when all our people, with many voices in one united chorus, will glorify your holy Name. *Amen.*

For Fellow Travelers

O God, the strength of your people in every moment of need: grant us so to pass through the coming days with faithful hearts and unfaltering purpose, that we may in all things prove worthy of the gift of your Son and bring the light of encouragement to our fellow travelers; through Jesus Christ our Lord. *Amen.*

For the World

Prayers for all nations and peoples of the world, for those living in conflict and those working toward peace, and for the whole creation

For the Human Family

O God, you made us in your own image and redeemed us through Jesus your Son: Look with compassion on the whole human family; take away the arrogance and hatred which infect our hearts; break down the walls that separate us; unite us in bonds of love; and work through our struggle and confusion to accomplish your purposes on earth; that, in your good time, all nations and races may serve you in harmony around your heavenly throne; through Jesus Christ our Lord. *Amen.*

✠

Show unto the nations, O Father of all, how to rise above the causes that divide us, and to seek in faith a world made one in the love of thee; that we may win our way to justice, freedom, and peace, not by might, nor by power, but by thy Spirit in Jesus Christ our Lord. *Amen.*

✠

God of Truth and Justice,
Unveil the truth that divides us.
Shred the fears that keep us silent.
Break the chains—of power, privilege, and pride—that blind us to the sacred worth of every human being.
Give us the audacity to speak, the strength to stand, and a love so fierce that no barrier can withstand it.
Until no one is master, no one is slave,
and all your people walk free in your Light.
Amen.

For All Who Need Help

We beg you, Lord, to help and to defend us. Deliver the oppressed, pity the insignificant, raise the fallen, show yourself to the needy, heal the sick, bring back those of your people who have gone astray, feed the hungry, lift up the weak, take off the prisoners' chains. May every nation come to know that you alone are God, that Jesus Christ is your Child, that we are your people, the sheep that you pasture. *Amen.* *– Clement of Rome (ca. 35-100)*

✠

We bring before you, O Lord,
  the troubles and perils of people and nations,
  the sighing of prisoners and captives,
  the sorrows of the bereaved,
  the necessities of strangers,
  the helplessness of the weak,
  the despondency of the weary,
  the failing powers of the aged.
O Lord, draw near to each,
for the sake of Jesus Christ our Lord. *Amen.*

– Anselm of Canterbury (1033-1109)

For Leaders Among the Nations

O Almighty God, kindle, we beseech thee, in every heart the true love of peace, and guide with thy wisdom those who take counsel for the nations of the earth, that in tranquillity thy dominion may increase till the earth is filled with the knowledge of thy love; through Jesus Christ our Lord, who liveth and reigneth with thee, in the unity of the Holy Spirit, one God, now and for ever. *Amen.*

For Just Nations

Almighty God our heavenly Father, guide the nations of the world into the way of justice and truth, and establish among them that peace which is the fruit of righteousness, that they may become the kingdom of our Lord and Savior Jesus Christ. *Amen.*

For Our Enemies

O God, the Father of all, whose Son commanded us to love our enemies: Lead them and us from prejudice to truth; deliver them and us from hatred, cruelty, and revenge; and in your good time enable us all to stand reconciled before you; through Jesus Christ our Lord. *Amen.*

For Peace

Lord, let us have no other God before you and let us seek no other peace but the peace which is yours. *Amen.*

For All Who Make Peace

God of justice and mercy, we pray for all who labor for peace: in families, communities, and nations. Strengthen those who choose repair over retaliation, and patience over power. Sustain those who work for peace without recognition or reward. Shape our lives toward justice and compassion. Make us people willing to listen, to examine our own complicity, and to practice humility. May peace take root among us in the presence of right relationship. *Amen.*

For Servant Hearts

O God, the King of righteousness, lead us, we pray you, in ways of justice and peace; inspire us to break down all tyranny and oppression, to gain for every person their due reward, and from every person their due service; that each may live for all and all may care for each, in Jesus Christ our Lord. *Amen.*

For People of Different Cultures

O God, who created all peoples in your image, we thank you for the wonderful diversity of races and cultures in this world. Enrich our lives by ever-widening circles of fellowship, and show us your presence in those who differ most from us, until our knowledge of your love is made perfect in our love for all your children; through Jesus Christ our Lord. *Amen.*

For Those Who Fight Oppression

Almighty God, who created us in your own image: Grant us grace fearlessly to contend against evil and to make no peace with oppression; and, that we may reverently use our freedom, help us to employ it in the maintenance of justice in our communities and among the nations, to the glory of your holy Name; through Jesus Christ our Lord, who lives and reigns with you and the Holy Spirit, one God, now and for ever. *Amen.*

For People of Other Faiths

Dear Father, bless people of all faiths and those of none, that all may be given greater sensitivity to those who are different, deeper understanding of traditions other than our own, and a strengthened determination to work together for the sake of the whole human family. *Amen.*

For Those Enslaved

Compassionate God,
Whose love set the people of Israel free
from slavery,
Give us wisdom and courage to listen and
fight for the rights of those who suffer
the consequences of modern slavery,
That we may all live free on earth as it will be
in your heavenly kingdom.
Through Jesus Christ, your Son our Redeemer.
Amen.

– Carlos Respeito, Diocese of Lebombo
Anglican Church of Mozambique and Angola

For Inhabitants of War-Torn Lands

We weep with you, Lord, for all those whose lives are ripped open by violence, oppression, and the horrors of war. The blood of the innocent cries out, and how can we keep silent? We beg you to beat swords into ploughshares, to end bloodshed, to feed the hungry, to care for the wounded, and above all to move in the hearts of leaders and bring peace to this broken world, in the name of the one pierced for us all, Jesus Christ our Lord. *Amen.*

For the Persecuted

Give salvation and strength, O King of saints, to those who, being persecuted for righteousness' sake, are in great tribulation. And grant that these your followers, loving not their lives unto the death and leaving all to follow you, may overcome by the word of their testimony, and overcoming, may inherit all things. *Amen.*

For the Oppressed

Look with pity, O heavenly Father, upon the people in this land who live with injustice, terror, disease, and death as their constant companions. Have mercy upon us. Help us to eliminate our cruelty to these our neighbors. Strengthen those who spend their lives establishing equal protection of the law and equal opportunities for all. And grant that every one of us may enjoy a fair portion of the riches of this land; through Jesus Christ our Lord. *Amen.*

For the United Nations

Eternal God, we pray for all who serve in the United Nations. Grant your blessing upon their endeavors to heal the wounds of the world through cooperation in education and other fields of human service. May your Holy Spirit so guide their deliberations in Council and Assembly, that all causes of strife may be removed, and peace and concord be secured among all peoples of the earth. *Amen.*

A Prayer for Immigrants

God of every journey,
you led your people through wilderness
and water,
into unfamiliar lands and uncertain futures.

We pray for immigrants:
for those who travel by choice
and those who move because there is no
other option.
Grant them safety on the road,
companionship in unfamiliar places,
and provision for each day.

Widen our hearts in the communities
they enter.
Let hospitality replace fear,
and justice shape welcome.
May their work be honored,
their voices heard,
and their lives rooted in dignity.

As new lives take shape,
may their homes reflect the way of Jesus
and the way of love.

Remain faithful to them,
in every land and season. *Amen.*

– Melissa Rau, Diocese of Southwest Florida

For Refugees

God our Creator: We ask for your loving presence and for your peace to be with refugees in our local communities and around the world. Be with all who are in fear. Be with those whose lives and livelihoods are under threat, and whose religious freedoms are being compromised. Be with us as we strive to enact your will in our welcome and support of refugees. Be with those in positions of leadership, that their decisions may bend toward peace and not division, and that they might realize the power they hold to do justice. Give us all strength and courage. Equip and empower us to be witnesses to your love, as advocates and as servants, as ministers of welcome and bearers of hope, especially for those seeking refuge. In your holy Name we pray. *Amen.*

– Twila Smith, Diocese of Oklahoma

For All Who Seek Deliverance

Liberating God, you once delivered the children of Israel from the tyrannical rule of Pharaoh and guided them to the promised land of justice and abundance: deliver your people today from all unjust rulers, so that, freed from all bondage and every oppression, we might follow our only Lord, Jesus Christ, who with you and the Holy Spirit, lives and reigns for ever and ever. *Amen.*

– Cody Maynus, Diocese of Minnesota

For the Kingdom

Creator, you are blessed, for you lift up the poor, fill the hungry, comfort the grieving, and heal the persecuted. Remind us that this world is temporary, and your city is forever, so that we may begin building with you the kingdom to come, in all its glory and peace. In the name of Jesus Christ, *Amen.*

– Cara Ellen Modisett
Diocese of Southwestern Virginia

For the Creation

O Loving Creator, you have always been, and before you nothing has been. The stars of the heavens, the grasses of the earth, the depths of the seas, sing out to you. Fill us with your light that we may have the strength to understand and the eyes to see. Teach us to walk the soft earth as relatives to your creation. Guide us, for without you we are nothing. *Amen.*

– Kurt Huber, Cheyenne River Episcopal Mission
Diocese of South Dakota

For Joy in God's Creation

O Heavenly Father, who hast filled the world with beauty; Open, we beseech thee, our eyes to behold thy gracious hand in all thy works; that rejoicing in thy whole creation, we may learn to serve thee with gladness; for the sake of him by whom all things were made, thy Son, Jesus Christ our Lord. *Amen.*

Confession of Sin Against Creation

Holy One, source of all life,
we confess that we have not cared for creation
as you entrusted it to us.

We have taken more than we need
and called it progress.
We have chosen convenience over
responsibility,
and distance over care.

Forgive us for the harm done
through neglect and excess,
and through systems we benefit from
yet fail to question.

Turn us again toward right relationship
with the earth and with one another.
Give us courage to change,
humility to learn,
and perseverance to act.

Renew us, O God,
and restore the face of the earth,
beginning with us. *Amen.*

– Melissa Rau, Diocese of Southwest Florida

God in All Things

Apprehend God in all things,
for God is in all things.
Every single creature is full of God,
and is a book about God.
Every creature is a word of God.
If I spent enough time with the tiniest
creature—even a caterpillar—
I would never have to prepare a sermon,
so full of God
is every creature.

– Meister Eckhart (ca. 1260-1328)

To Serve God in Creation

O God, of whose gift come sunshine, and friendship, and the glory of a summer's day; who in the common things of daily life givest to us thy very self, making of bread and wine the sacrament of thy sustaining presence; strengthen and refresh us, that we may seek thee eagerly, find thee surely, and serve thee faithfully, through Jesus Christ our Lord. *Amen.*

To Love God's Creation

O Creator, help me to love all of your creation, the whole and every grain of sand in it. Let me love every leaf, every ray of God's light. Let me love the animals, love the plants, love everything. Loving everything, I will perceive the divine mystery in things. Once I perceive it, may I begin to comprehend it better every day. And may I come at last to love the whole world with an all-embracing love. *Amen.*

– Adapted from Fyodor Dostoevsky (1821–1881)

A Prayer for Change

Come, Holy Spirit, come; come as the wind and cleanse; come as the fire and burn; come from the four winds and turn the hearts and minds of these your servants, to their great good and to your great glory; who with the Father and the Son are one God, now and for ever. *Amen.*

For the Church Universal

Prayers for the Church worldwide, for all Christians, and for the coming of the Kingdom

For the Church Universal

Almighty God, you sent your Son Jesus Christ to reconcile the world to yourself: We praise and bless you for those whom you have sent in the power of the Spirit to preach the Gospel to all nations. We thank you that in all parts of the earth a community of love has been gathered together by their prayers and labors, and that in every place your servants call upon your Name; for the kingdom and the power and the glory are yours for ever. *Amen.*

✠

Gracious Father, we pray for thy holy Catholic Church. Fill it with all truth, in all truth with all peace. Where it is corrupt, purify it; where it is in error, direct it; where in any thing it is amiss, reform it. Where it is right, strengthen it; where it is in want, provide for it; where it is divided, reunite it; for the sake of Jesus Christ thy Son our Savior. *Amen.*

✠

O God, the creator and preserver of all mankind, we humbly beseech thee for all sorts and conditions of men; that thou wouldest be pleased to make thy ways known unto them, thy saving health unto all nations. More especially we pray for thy holy Church universal; that it may be so guided and governed by thy good Spirit, that all who profess and call themselves Christians may be led into the way of truth, and hold the faith in unity of spirit, in the bond of peace, and in righteousness of life. Finally, we commend to thy fatherly goodness all those who are in any ways afflicted or distressed, in mind, body, or estate; [especially those for whom our prayers are desired]; that it may please thee to comfort and relieve them according to their several necessities, giving them patience under their sufferings, and a happy issue out of all their afflictions. And this we beg for Jesus Christ's sake. *Amen.*

✠

O Lord Christ, whose Kingdom is not in word but in power, grant that even as we desire your appearing among peoples, we may labor and pay our part of the cost, by the help of your Holy Spirit. *Amen.*

✠

Keep, O Lord, your household the Church in your steadfast faith and love, that through your grace we may proclaim your truth with boldness, and minister your justice with compassion; for the sake of our Savior Jesus Christ, who lives and reigns with you and the Holy Spirit, one God, now and for ever. *Amen.*

For Unity

O God, in whose image we are made, and in whose earthly family there is neither Jew nor Greek, male nor female, bond nor free: Enliven your church with your love that we may show to the world the unity to which you have called it in the gospel of your Son, Jesus Christ our Lord. *Amen.*

For Evangelists

Spirit of fire, descend with power upon all who speak the name of Jesus. Burn out all heresies, hatred, small-mindedness, and fear, to make us bold and truthful witnesses to your Gospel. Purify our lips and our lives, that we may speak Christ not only in our words, but also in our actions. May our lives be loud with the life-giving truth of Jesus Christ, in whose holy Name we pray. *Amen.*

For Those Who Preach the Gospel

Let your Word burn upon my lips, O Lord. Let my words ignite the hearts and minds of your people. May your Gospel be, this day, the fire that burns but does not consume; may it be the living water that quenches a deeper thirst. And may I, a servant of this Gospel, be a vessel of its power and a witness to its grace. I ask all this through Christ, the Word incarnate. *Amen.*

– Phil Hooper, Diocese of Southern Ohio

For Courageous Witnesses

Thou who art heroic love, keep alive in our hearts that adventurous spirit, which makes men scorn the way of safety, so that Thy will be done. *Amen.*

For the Forward Movement of the Church

We pray Thee, O God, for Thy blessing upon the Forward Movement of Thy Church. Use it, we beseech Thee, to open our eyes to the needs of men for the Gospel of Christ, and to the opportunities that lie before the Church to extend His Kingdom. Stir up, O Lord, the wills of all Thy people to share in this work of gladness of heart and self sacrificing spirit; and let not our purpose slack until the kingdoms of this world have become the Kingdom of our God and of His Christ. *Amen.*

For All the Faithful

Lord of all power and might, the author and giver of all good things: Graft in our hearts the love of your Name; increase in us true religion; nourish us with all goodness; and bring forth in us the fruit of good works. *Amen.*

For Servants of God

Teach us, good Lord, to serve Thee as Thou deservest; to give and not to count the cost; to fight and not to heed the wounds; to toil and not to seek for rest; to labor and not to ask for any reward, save that of knowing that we do Thy will; through Jesus Christ our Lord. *Amen.*

– Ignatius of Loyola (1491–1556)

For Christ-Like Lives

You have showed us, O Lord, what is good: enable us, we pray, to perform what you require, even to do justice, to love kindness, and to walk humbly with our God. *Amen.*

For Zealous Followers of Christ

Almighty God, whose Son Jesus Christ came to cast fire upon the earth, grant that by the prayers of Thy faithful people a fire of burning zeal may be kindled and pass from heart to heart, that the light of Thy Church may shine forth bright and clear; through the same Thy Son Jesus Christ our Lord. *Amen.*

For the Whole Church

O Eternal God, who by Thy Son Jesus Christ didst establish the family of Thy Church in all the world; Breathe upon it anew the gifts of Thy Holy Spirit, that, awakening to Thy command, it may go forth in lowly service yet in conquering might to win mankind to the love of Thy Name; through our only Savior Jesus Christ. *Amen.*

For a General Convention

Almighty and everlasting God, who by thy Holy Spirit didst preside in the Council of the blessed Apostles, and hast promised, through thy Son Jesus Christ, to be with thy Church to the end of the world; We beseech thee to be with the Council of thy Church here assembled in thy Name and Presence. Save us from all error, ignorance, pride, and prejudice; and of thy great mercy vouchsafe, we beseech thee, so to direct, sanctify, and govern us in our work, by the mighty power of the Holy Ghost, that the comfortable Gospel of Christ may be truly preached, truly received, and truly followed, in all places, to the breaking down the kingdom of sin, Satan, and death; till at length the whole of thy dispersed sheep, being gathered into one fold, shall become partakers of everlasting life; through the merits and death of Jesus Christ our Savior. *Amen.*

For All Orders of Clergy

Almighty God, the giver of all good gifts, in your divine providence you have appointed various orders in your Church: Give your grace, we humbly pray, to all who are [now] called to any office and ministry for your people; and so fill them with the truth of your doctrine and clothe them with holiness of life, that they may faithfully serve before you, to the glory of your great Name and for the benefit of your holy Church; through Jesus Christ our Lord, who lives and reigns with you, in the unity of the Holy Spirit, one God, now and for ever. *Amen.*

✠

Quicken, O Lord, we pray, all members of your church, that they may be alive to the opportunities and responsibilities of our time. *Amen.*

For Future Clergy

O God, you led your holy apostles to ordain ministers in every place: Grant that your Church, under the guidance of the Holy Spirit, may choose suitable persons for the ministry of Word and Sacrament, and may uphold them in their work for the extension of your kingdom; through him who is the Shepherd and Bishop of our souls, Jesus Christ our Lord, who lives and reigns with you and the Holy Spirit, one God, for ever and ever. *Amen.*

For Monastic Orders

O Lord Jesus Christ, you became poor for our sake, that we might be made rich through your poverty: Guide and sanctify, we pray, those whom you call to follow you under the vows of poverty, chastity, and obedience, that by their prayer and service they may enrich your Church, and by their life and worship may glorify your Name; for you reign with the Father and the Holy Spirit, one God, now and for ever. *Amen.*

For Campus Ministers

O Lord our Gardener, equip your laborers with every good thing as they sow the good news of your love at colleges and universities across this land. Give them humility and wisdom to find new ways to use what has grown old, and open their hearts to the wonder and worries of their students. Form them into strong, loving, and wise mentors. Give them trust and perseverance when the soil is hard and rocky; grant them satisfaction when the fruit of their labor has ripened. Send them wise and understanding bishops and colleagues to water and fertilize their efforts. Bring the students they serve to maturity and to a vibrant trust in the goodness of your Son and his Church, that they may have a foretaste of the feast prepared from the dawn of time by the goodness of Jesus Christ our Savior. *Amen.*

– Noah Stansbury, Diocese of Texas

For One Who Has Lost Faith

God of Job and Thomas, you know the questions that trouble our hearts, the doubts that keep us awake in the night. We ask you to draw near to those who have lost their faith and given up their hope in you. Help them to know—or know again—that they do not walk alone: through the promise of your holy Word, the revelation of your created world, and the love of the fellow children of God who walk the path beside them. Let us be the light that draws them back to you, the true Light of all. We pray in the name of Jesus, who wept in the garden and knows all our grief. *Amen.*

For Growth in the Spiritual Life

Grant us, O Lord, to understand the gift of prayer: that we may pray effectually for everyone we try to help.

Grant us the wisdom of a loving heart, ever patient and wondrous kind.

Grant us that strong sense of duty which refuses to yield to the inclination of the moment.

Grant us the royal gift of courage; that we may do each disagreeable duty at once.

Grant us a true sense of humor; may its kindly light and healing power relax life's tension.

O Lord Jesus Christ, who has taught us always to pray and not to faint, we lift always to Thy mercy the needs of Thy Church. And since Thou hast given us the resolve to go forward and not back, grant to our leaders to be both wise and daring disciples, and to thy people an heart to follow them, for Thy sake who art with the Father and the Holy Spirit one God, world without end. *Amen.*

For the Faithful Departed

Eternal Lord God, you hold all souls in life: Give to your whole Church in paradise and on earth your light and your peace; and grant that we, following the good examples of those who have served you here and are now at rest, may at the last enter with them into your unending joy; through Jesus Christ our Lord, who lives and reigns with you, in the unity of the Holy Spirit, one God, now and for ever. *Amen.*

For the Sick & Suffering

Prayers for all who sorrow,
in our own lives and
around the world

For the Fearful

Lord Jesus, when your disciples were tossed and tormented by a terrifying storm, you came to them with great calm, and they were safe. Speak peace, we pray you, to those who are in agony of mind or body; that even when pain and fatigue threatens to overwhelm them, they may find rest to their souls and to their bodies; grant them to drink deeply of the fountain of life that is in you and that gives hope and healing evermore. *Amen.*

For Those Who Are Anxious

Most loving Father, whose will it is for us to give thanks for all things, to fear nothing but the loss of you, and to cast all our care on you who care for us: Preserve us from faithless fears and worldly anxieties, that no clouds of this mortal life may hide from us the light of that love which is immortal, and which you have manifested to us in your Son Jesus Christ our Lord; who lives and reigns with you, in the unity of the Holy Spirit, one God, now and for ever. *Amen.*

For All in Need

God of love, God of mercy, you said that you would be with us to the end. Be with all of us who are suffering and in need of your love and compassion. *Amen.*

–Annie Kate Jacobs, Diocese of East Carolina

For the Lost

O Lord Jesus Christ, Thou, good Shepherd of the sheep, who camest to seek the lost, and to gather them to Thy fold, have compassion upon those who have wandered from Thee; feed those who hunger, cause the weary to lie down in Thy pastures, bind up those who are broken in heart, and strengthen those who are weak, that we, relying on Thy care and being comforted by Thy love, may abide in Thy guidance to our lives' end; for Thy name's sake. *Amen.*

For All Who Sorrow

Creator, you know our hearts and share our sorrows. The news (*of…*) brings an emptiness into our lives. We pray for relatives, friends, and neighbors. Be gentle with us in our fear and anxiety, comfort us in our sorrow, strengthen us with hope, and breathe peace into our troubled hearts. When we are tormented by guilt or despair, help us to feel your mercy and love. When we are angry at the situation we have sustained, grant those around us a compassionate heart. When we long for words of comfort, yet find them hard to hear, grant those around us a calming presence. Creator, give us courage and strength to meet the days ahead in the comfort and knowledge of eternal life with you and all our relatives. *Mitakuye Oyasin. Amen.*

– *Shaneequa Brokenleg, Diocese of South Dakota*

For Sufferers

O merciful Father, who hast taught us in thy holy Word that thou dost not willingly afflict or grieve the children of men: Look with pity upon the sorrows of thy servant for whom our prayers are offered. Remember *him*, O Lord, in mercy, nourish *his* soul with patience, comfort *him* with a sense of thy goodness, lift up thy countenance upon *him*, and give *him* peace; through Jesus Christ our Lord. *Amen.*

✠

O Lord who dost feel the pain of the world, look down upon all sick and suffering persons; enfold them with thy love, that in the midst of pain they may find thy presence; to doctors and nurses grant tender hearts and healing hands; and give health again in body and soul, for thy tender mercy's sake. *Amen.*

Lord Jesus Christ, Good Shepherd of the sheep, you gather the lambs in your arms and carry them in your bosom: We commend to your loving care this child, *N.* Relieve *her* pain, guard *her* from all danger, restore to *her* your gifts of gladness and strength, and raise *her* up to a life of service to you. Hear us, we pray, for your dear Name's sake. *Amen.*

For Those in Chronic Pain

Eternal Gentleness, give me the courage to remember that you are not separate from a body that experiences pain. I am loved because I exist. There is no earning grace, there is nothing that I must do to earn your love and power. Remind me that you are here with me, in this pain, until I reach the other side. Let me rest in your compassion. *Amen.*

– Ruth Marston-Bihl
United Methodist Church, Seattle, WA

For the Weary

God of our life,
there are days when the burdens we carry
chafe our shoulders and weigh us down;
when the road seems dreary and endless,
the skies gray and threatening;
when our lives have no music in them,
and our hearts are lonely.
Flood the path with light,
run our eyes to where
the skies are full of promise;
tune our hearts to brave music;
give us the sense of comradeship
with heroes and saints of every age;
and so quicken our spirits
that we may be able to encourage
the souls of all who journey with us
on the road of life, to your honor and glory.
Amen.

For Those Facing Surgery

Strengthen your servant *N.*, O God, to do what *he* has to do and bear what *he* has to bear; that, accepting your healing gifts through the skill of surgeons and nurses, *he* may be restored to usefulness in your world with a thankful heart; through Jesus Christ our Lord. *Amen.*

For Caregivers for the Sick

God, our refuge and strength, our present help in time of trouble, care for those who tend the needs of *N.* Strengthen them in body and spirit. Refresh them when weary; console them when anxious; comfort them in grief; and hearten them in discouragement. Be with us all, and give us peace at all times and in every way, through Christ our peace. *Amen.*

For Those Living with Terminal Diagnosis

This is a path I do not know how to travel, Lord. This is not where I thought my journey would lead. But I trust in this: that you walk beside me even now along this unexpected byway. I know that you will be with me all the way to the road's end; that you will open the gate at the shadow-dappled edge of life and guide me into the meadowlands beyond. Until then, help me to notice; to cherish; and to name what is beautiful and precious in this world. Guide me gently, Good Shepherd, and watch over the ones I love. *Amen.*

– Phil Hooper, Diocese of Southern Ohio

For Those Seeking Healing

Loving God, we thank you for your loving knowledge of who we are and how we are made. In Jesus you know the damage that can be done to our bodies, our minds and our spirits when we are mistreated by others. You know what it is to be humiliated, shamed, and forsaken. We bring to you our whole selves: body, mind, and spirit. We pray that where there is hurt you will heal us; where we are broken you will make us whole; where there is shame and self-loathing, you will restore dignity, self-acceptance, and a knowledge of ourselves as your beloved children; where there is loneliness and isolation, pour out your Holy Spirit to make known to us your loving presence in our lives. We thank you that we are wonderfully made and we ask you to restore in us unity of body, mind, and spirit within the love of our Lord Jesus Christ. *Amen.*

For Those in Grief

Most merciful God, whose wisdom is beyond our understanding, deal graciously with *NN.* in *their* grief. Surround *them* with your love, that *they* may not be overwhelmed by *their* loss, but have confidence in your goodness, and strength to meet the days to come; through Jesus Christ our Lord. *Amen.*

For Those in Recovery

O Lord, your compassions never fail and your mercies are new every morning: We give you thanks for giving our brother (sister) *N.* both relief from pain and hope of health renewed. Continue in *him*, we pray, the good work you have begun; that *he*, daily increasing in bodily strength, and rejoicing in your goodness, may so order *his* life and conduct that *he* may always think and do those things that please you; through Jesus Christ our Lord. *Amen.*

For the Loss of a Child

O Lord Jesus Christ, who for us was born as an infant in Bethlehem, we commit to your loving care this child: Call *her* to yourself, send your holy angels to lead *her* gently to the heavenly habitations of perpetual peace and joy, and hold *her* in the everlasting arms of your unfailing love. *Amen.*

For Our Lost

We give back to you, O God, those whom you gave to us. You did not lose them when you gave them to us, and we do not lose them by their return to you. Your dear Son has taught us that life is eternal and love cannot die. So death is only a horizon, and a horizon is only the limit of our sight. Open our eyes to see more clearly, and draw us closer to you that we may know that we are nearer to our loved ones who are with you. You have told us that you are preparing a place for us: prepare us also for that happy place, that where you are we may also be always, O dear Lord of life and death. *Amen.*

– William Penn (1644-1718)

For Those Grieving the Loss of a Pet

Loving God, you brought this beloved animal into the life of *N.* to share kindness, joy, and faithful companionship: Receive our thanks and praise for the community between your animals and your people, and all the ways in which we bless each other's lives; in your goodness, Blessed Creator, hear our prayer. *Amen.*

For the Poor

Almighty and most merciful God, we remember before you all poor and neglected persons whom it would be easy for us to forget: the homeless and the destitute, the old and the sick, and all who have none to care for them. Help us to heal those who are broken in body or spirit, and to turn their sorrow into joy. Grant this, Father, for the love of your Son, who for our sake became poor, Jesus Christ our Lord. *Amen.*

For the Homeless and Orphaned

Lord Jesus, who in the days of thy flesh hadst no place to lay thy head, look, we beseech thee, with compassion upon all homeless folk and all children left without parental care. And that we do not fail them in their loneliness and need, inflame the hearts of our people with a spirit of concern for their welfare. Bless all homes for orphans, and all organizations working for the relief of human distress; and this we ask for thy Name's sake. *Amen.*

For Those in Crisis

Holy One, you are our comfort and strength in times of sudden disaster, crisis, or chaos. Surround us now with your grace and peace through storm or earthquake, fire or flood. By your Spirit, lift up those who have fallen, sustain those who work to rescue or rebuild, and fill us with the hope of your new creation; through you, our rock and redeemer. *Amen.*

For Those in Prison

Lord Jesus, for our sake you were condemned as a criminal: Visit our jails and prisons with your pity and judgment. Remember all prisoners, and bring the guilty to repentance and amendment of life according to your will, and give them hope for their future. When any are held unjustly, bring them release; forgive us, and teach us to improve our justice. Remember those who work in these institutions; keep them humane and compassionate; and save them from becoming brutal or callous. And since what we do for those in prison, O Lord, we do for you, constrain us to improve their lot. All this we ask for your mercy's sake. *Amen.*

✠

O God, who sparest when we deserve punishment, and in thy wrath rememberest mercy; We humbly beseech thee, of thy goodness, to comfort and succour all prisoners [especially those who are condemned to die]. Give them a right understanding of themselves, and of thy promises; that, trusting wholly in thy mercy, they may not place their confidence anywhere but in thee. Relieve the distressed, protect the innocent, awaken the guilty; and forasmuch as thou alone bringest light out of darkness, and good out of evil, grant to these thy servants, that by the power of thy Holy Spirit they may be set free from the chains of sin, and may be brought to newness of life; through Jesus Christ our Lord. *Amen.*

For Those Struggling with Addiction

O blessed Lord, you ministered to all who came to you: Look with compassion upon all who through addiction have lost their health and freedom. Restore to them the assurance of your unfailing mercy; remove from them the fears that beset them; strengthen them in the work of their recovery; and to those who care for them, give patient understanding and persevering love. *Amen.*

For Those Affected by Natural Disaster

Author of Creation, whose Spirit hovered over the waters before all things were and who spoke each thing into being: as disasters have torn apart the land and upended lives, speak into the swirling chaos of this moment your words of peace over anxiousness, of comfort over sorrow, of companionship over isolation, of hope over despondency, and of possibility over desolation, that we might glimpse and embody your recreative power, which draws all things to your very self and makes all things new. *Amen.*

– Caroline Hamilton-Arnold
Disciples of Christ, Houston, TX

For Refugees and the Homeless

Loving Jesus, you walked the roads of ancient Palestine and befriended the poor and outcast: Remember your brothers and sisters deprived of home and country, who search for refuge in the burning heat of the sun, the freezing cold of the sea, the humid heat of the forest, and the barren streets of alien cities. Still the storms that beset them, loving Jesus, and move our hearts to embrace them as our brothers and sisters and as fellow bearers of the Creator's divine image, that their anguish may be lifted and their sorrow turned to joy. *Amen.*

For the Marginalized

Almighty and most merciful God, we remember before you all poor and neglected persons whom it would be easy for us to forget: the homeless and the destitute, the old and the sick, and all who have none to care for them. Help us to heal those who are broken in body or spirit, and to turn their sorrow into joy. Grant this, Father, for the love of your Son, who for our sake became poor, Jesus Christ our Lord. *Amen.*

For Those Who Suffer from Abuse and Violence

Holy One, you do not distance yourself from the pain of your people, but in Jesus you bear that pain with all who suffer at others' hands. With your cleansing love bring healing and strength to *N.*; and by your justice, lift *him* up, that in body, mind and spirit, *he* may again rejoice. In Jesus' name we pray. *Amen.*

For Communities in Trouble

Out of the depths, we cry to you, God. Out of our suffering, our pain, our tears, we long for comfort. Out of our fear, our confusion, our anxiety, we long for guidance. Out of our anger, our frustration, our outrage, we long for justice. Rise up and save us, O God, for the sake of your steadfast love. *Amen.*

Salve Regina

Hail, holy Queen, Mother of Mercy,
our life, our sweetness and our hope.
To thee do we cry, poor banished children
of Eve;
to thee do we send up our sighs,
mourning and weeping in this valley of tears.
Turn then, most gracious advocate,
thine eyes of mercy toward us;
and after this our exile,
show unto us the blessed fruit of thy womb,
Jesus.
O clement, O loving, O sweet Virgin Mary.
Pray for us O holy Mother of God,
that we may be made worthy of the
promises of Christ. *Amen.*

Other Prayers

Lord, revive your church,
beginning with me.

Praise & Thanksgiving

The Divine Praises

Blessed be God.
Blessed be the holy and undivided Trinity.
Blessed be God the Father,
maker of heaven and earth.
Blessed be Jesus Christ,
true God and true Man.
Blessed be Jesus Christ
in his death and resurrection.
Blessed be Jesus Christ
on his throne of glory.
Blessed be Jesus Christ
in the Sacrament of his body and blood.
Blessed be God the Holy Spirit,
the Lord and giver of life.
Blessed be God in the Virgin Mary,
Mother of our God.
Blessed be God in Joseph,
guardian of the Incarnate Word.
Blessed be God in all the angels and saints.
Blessed be God.
Amen.

✠

Holy God,
Holy and mighty,
Holy immortal one,
Have mercy upon us. *Amen.*

Fourth-Century Hymn

May none of God's wonderful works
keep silence
night or morning.
Bright stars,
high mountains,
the depths of the seas,
sources of rushing rivers:
may all these break into song as we sing
to Father, Son and Holy Spirit.
May all the angels in the heavens reply:
Amen! Amen! Amen!
Power, praise, honor,
eternal glory to God,
the only giver of grace.
Amen! Amen! Amen!

Lord God, All Good

You are holy, Lord,
the only God,
and Your deeds are wonderful.
You are strong.
You are great.
You are the Most High.
You are Almighty.
You, Holy Father
are King of heaven and earth.
You are Three and One,
Lord God, all Good.
You are Good,
all Good, supreme Good,
Lord God, living and true.
You are love.
You are wisdom.
You are humility.
You are endurance.
You are rest.
You are peace.
You are joy and gladness.
You are justice and moderation.
You are all our riches,

and You suffice for us.
You are beauty.
You are gentleness.
You are our protector.
You are our guardian and defender.
You are our courage.
You are our haven and our hope.
You are our faith,
our great consolation.
You are our eternal life,
Great and Wonderful Lord,
God Almighty,
Merciful Saviour. *Amen.*

– Francis of Assisi (ca. 1181-1226)

God's Blessings

He turns darkness into light,
He changes sorrows into joy.
He strengthens the weak and makes us strong.
He reminds us daily of his love.
We are blessed.
We are blessed.
We are truly blessed. *Amen.*

– Kathy Lenox, Diocese of Western Oregon

God of Hope

O God of hope,
We thank you for the miracle of growth:
Growth of our gardens, plants, flowers,
Growth of our spirit, wisdom, courage.
O God of hope,
We thank you.
Amen.

– Barb Hagen, Diocese of Wisconsin

I Am Thankful

I am thankful for you.
I am thankful for the sunshine.
I am thankful for my faith.
I am thankful for yesterday.
I am thankful for today.
I am thankful for the setting sun.
I am thankful for tomorrow.
I am thankful.
Amen.

– Alice Briscoe Brown, Diocese of Pennsylvania

A General Thanksgiving

Accept, O Lord, our thanks and praise for all that you have done for us. We thank you for the splendor of the whole creation, for the beauty of this world, for the wonder of life, and for the mystery of love.

We thank you for the blessing of family and friends, and for the loving care which surrounds us on every side.

We thank you for setting us at tasks which demand our best efforts, and for leading us to accomplishments which satisfy and delight us.

We thank you also for those disappointments and failures that lead us to acknowledge our dependence on you alone.

Above all, we thank you for your Son Jesus Christ; for the truth of his Word and the example of his life; for his steadfast obedience, by which he overcame temptation; for his dying, through which he overcame death; and for his rising to life again, in which we are raised to the life of your kingdom.

Grant us the gift of your Spirit, that we may know him and make him known; and through him, at all times and in all places, may give thanks to you in all things. *Amen.*

An Act of Adoration

Worthy art thou, O God, to receive the honor and the power; for thou didst create all things, and because of thy will they are and were created.
Glory be to thee, O God.

Glory to thee O Christ, who didst redeem with thy love men of every kindred and tongue and people and nation.
Glory be to thee, O Christ.

Glory to thee, O Holy Spirit, for thy work in the Church, which will not cease until thou hast made of all mankind one family, to the praise and glory of God.
Glory be to thee, O Holy Spirit.
Amen.

An Act of Homage

To our Risen and Ascended Lord

Glory to Thee, O Christ, our ascended and ever present Lord, through whom we have access to the Father.

Glory to Thee who loves us and hast loosed us from our sins.

Glory to Thee who hast reconciled us all in one Body unto God through Thy Cross, so that we are no more strangers and sojourners but fellow citizens with the saints in the household of God.

Glory to Thee who has led captivity captive, and hast given gifts for the perfecting of Thy saints.

Glory to Thee who dost redeem unto God with Thy blood men of every title and tongue and people and nation.

Glory to Thee who art with us always, even unto the end of the world.

Glory to Thee who didst institute a perpetual remembrance of Thy precious death and dost unite us therein with Thy very self.

Glory to Thee who art in our midst when we are gathered together in Thy name.

Glory to Thee who hast gone before to prepare a place for us in Thy Father's house.

Glory to Thee, the author and finisher of our faith, that God in all things may be glorified. Amen.

Holy Spirit

Holy Spirit,
bestowing life unto life,
moving in All.
You are the root of all creatures,
washing away all impurity,
scouring guilt,
and anointing wounds.
Thus you are luminous and praiseworthy,
Life, awakening,
and re-awakening all that is. *Amen.*

– Hildegard of Bingen (1098-1179)

✠

Before thee, Father,
In righteousness and humility,
With thee, Brother,
In faith and courage,
In thee, Spirit,
In stillness. *Amen.*

– *Dag Hammarskjöld (1905–1961)*

The Prayer of Jesus

Holy One, our only Home,
hallowed be your name.
May your day dawn,
your will be done,
here as in heaven.
Feed us today,
and forgive us as we forgive each other.
Do not forsake us at the test,
but deliver us from evil.
For the glory, the power,
and the mercy are yours,
now and forever. *Amen.*

– *Martha Blacklock, Mother Thunder Mission*

Not Mine

Hallowed be Thy name,
    not mine,
Thy kingdom come,
    not mine,
Thy will be done,
    not mine,
Give us peace with Thee
    Peace with men
    Peace with ourselves,
And free us from all fear. *Amen.*

– Dag Hammarskjöld (1905–1961)

A Prayer of Self-Dedication

Almighty and eternal God, so draw our hearts to you, so guide our minds, so fill our imagination, so control our wills, that we may be wholly yours, utterly dedicated to you; and then use us, we pray, as you will, and always to your glory and the welfare of your people; through our Lord and Savior Jesus Christ. *Amen.*

Daily Devotions

On Waking

I praise my God this day.
I give myself to God this day.
I ask God to help me this day.
Amen.

✠

Holy One, by your grace help me to receive the gifts of this day, and fulfill your commandment of love, with gladness, simplicity, and singleness of heart, through Christ our Lord. *Amen.*

– Regina Walton, Diocese of Massachusetts

✠

O Lord Thou knowest how busy I must be this day; if I forget Thee, do not Thou forget me. *Amen.*

– Jacob Astley (1579–1652)

A Morning Prayer

Thou art my God, and I will thank thee; Thou art my God, and I will praise thee. *Amen.*

A Daily Dedication

God helping me, I will do my best, with what I am, where I am today for Jesus Christ.

Thou knowest, O God, the duties that lie before us this day, the dangers that may confront us, that sins that may beset us; guide us, strengthen us, protect us. Give us Thy power, that we may become a power for righteousness among our fellows. Give us Thy love, that all lesser things may have no attraction for us; that selfishness, impurity, and falseness may drop away as dead desires, holding no meaning for us; for Jesus Christ's sake. *Amen.*

A Morning Litany

In the name of the Father, and of the Son, and of the Holy Ghost. *Amen.*

Come Holy Ghost, fill the hearts of thy faithful people,
and kindle in them the fire of thy love.

Holy Father, strength of thy children by night and by day, *have mercy upon us.*

Blessed Jesus, our food and our strength, sweet spirit, light and guide of our souls,
have mercy upon us.

Holy Trinity, abyss of love,
have mercy upon us.
Holy, blessed, and glorious Trinity,
I adore thee.
In thy perfect beauty, *I adore thee.*
In thy boundless power, *I adore thee.*
With the Blessed Virgin Mary, *I adore thee.*
With the holy angels, *I adore thee.*
With the blessed saints, *I adore thee.*

In union with every Eucharist offered today,
I adore thee.
Praise and thanksgiving for protection during the past night, *I offer thee.*
Praise and thanksgiving for all thy mercies and blessings, *I offer thee.*
My daily work, *I offer thee.*
All my thoughts, *I offer thee.*
All my words, *I offer thee.*
All my deeds, *I offer thee.*
My joys and consolations, *I offer thee.*
My sorrows and troubles, *I offer thee.*
My difficulties, doubts, and anxieties,
I offer thee.

On all near and dear to me, especially…
send thy blessing, O Lord.
On every person I will encounter this day,
send thy blessing, O Lord.
On the nations and those in authority,
send thy blessing, O Lord.
On all caught in war, famine, or disaster,
send thy blessing, O Lord.
On those who protect our nation and cities,
send thy blessing, O Lord.

On the Church throughout the world,
send thy blessing, O Lord.
On my parish and diocese, its clergy and people, *send thy blessing, O Lord.*
On schools, colleges, universities, and seminaries, *send thy blessing, O Lord.*
On religious orders, *send thy blessing, O Lord.*
On those in danger by reason of labor or travel, *send thy blessing, O Lord.*
On homes and families, children and parents, *send thy blessing, O Lord.*
On those who are lonely or bereaved,
send thy blessing, O Lord.
On those who are ill and in pain, and all who care for them, *send thy blessing, O Lord.*

To all who will die this day,
give true contrition and receive their souls.
To the faithful departed,
grant light and peace.

In my daily temptations,
Good Lord, deliver me.
When I forget thee,
recall me to thyself.

In any danger of soul or body,
preserve and defend me.

May the Blessed Mother and all the saints pray for me and the angels surround and protect me; may my soul this day be made more fit, for the Day which has no end; through Jesus Christ our Lord. *Amen.*

For Facing the Day

Holy One, through your persistent grace, help me this day to bear Christ's image within myself; to bear witness to Christ's love in the world; and to bear the sufferings of others, willingly, bravely, and with compassion. Strengthen and guide me by your Holy Spirit. *Amen.*

– *Regina Walton, Diocese of Massachusetts*

For Today

O God: Give me strength to live another day; Let me not turn coward before its difficulties or prove recreant to its duties; Let me not lose faith in other people; Keep me sweet and sound of heart, in spite of ingratitude, treachery, or meanness; Preserve me from minding little stings or giving them; Help me to keep my heart clean, and to live so honestly and fearlessly that no outward failure can dishearten me or take away the joy of conscious integrity; Open wide the eyes of my soul that I may see good in all things; Grant me this day some new vision of thy truth; Inspire me with the spirit of joy and gladness; and make me the cup of strength to suffering souls; in the name of the strong Deliverer, our only Lord and Savior, Jesus Christ. *Amen.*

– Phillips Brooks (1835–1893)

For Grace

O Lord, our heavenly Father, almighty and everlasting God, who hast safely brought us to the beginning of this day: Defend us in the same with thy mighty power; and grant that this day we fall into no sin, neither run into any kind of danger; but that we, being ordered by thy governance, may do always what is righteous in thy sight; through Jesus Christ our Lord. *Amen.*

In the Evening

Holy One, draw near to me, now it is night.
I turn out my pockets of all cares and concerns,
and trust them to your good keeping.
Forgive my sins.
Renew me with sleep.
Accept my thanks for this day past.
Continue my conversion,
tomorrow and forevermore. *Amen.*

– *Regina Walton, Diocese of Massachusetts*

✠

I give God thanks for all that was good in the day that is ending.
I ask God's mercy on my sins and omissions this day.
I seek God's peace in my home and in all the world this night. *Amen.*

For the Presence of Christ

Lord Jesus, stay with us, for evening is at hand and the day is past; be our companion in the way, kindle our hearts, and awaken hope, that we may know you as you are revealed in Scripture and the breaking of bread. Grant this for the sake of your love. *Amen.*

✠

Be our light in the darkness, O Lord, and in your great mercy defend us from all perils and dangers of this night; for the love of your only Son, our Savior Jesus Christ. *Amen.*

✠

Keep watch, dear Lord, with those who work, or watch, or weep this night, and give your angels charge over those who sleep. Tend the sick, Lord Christ; give rest to the weary, bless the dying, soothe the suffering, pity the afflicted, shield the joyous; and all for your love's sake. *Amen.*

At Night

I will lay me down in peace and take my rest: for Thou, Lord, only, makest us to dwell in safety.

Thou, O Christ, art in the midst of us and we are called by Thy name; leave us not, O Lord, our God.

Save us, O Lord, while waking, guard us while sleeping; that awake we may watch with Christ and asleep we may rest in peace. *Amen.*

Nunc Dimittis, for Justice

Let justice roll down like waters,
and righteousness like an ever-flowing stream.

Now, Lord, you let your servant go in peace:
your word has been fulfilled.

My own eyes have seen the salvation which you have prepared in the sight of every people;

A light to reveal you to the nations
and the glory of your people Israel.

Glory to the Father and to the Son and to the Holy Spirit; as it was in the beginning is now and shall be for ever. *Amen.*

Let justice roll down like waters,
and righteousness like an ever-flowing stream.

Abide with Us

Abide with us, O Lord,
for it is toward evening
and the day is far spent;
abide with us, and with Thy whole Church.

Abide with us in the evening of the day,
in the evening of life,
in the evening of the world.

Abide with us in Thy grace and mercy,
in holy Word and Sacrament,
in Thy comfort and Thy blessing.

Abide with us in the night of distress and fear,
in the night of doubt and temptation,
in the night of bitter death,
when these shall overtake us.

Abide with us and with all Thy faithful ones,
O Lord,
in time and in eternity.
In Jesus' name. *Amen.*

– Georg Christian Dieffenbach (1822–1901)

Phos Hilaron

O gracious light, pure brightness of the everliving Father in heaven, O Jesus Christ, holy and blessed!

Now as we come to the setting of the sun, and our eyes behold the vesper light, we sing your praises, O God: Father, Son, and Holy Spirit.

You are worthy at all times to be praised by happy voices, O Son of God, O Giver of Life, and to be glorified through all the worlds. *Amen.*

For Protection

Blessed are you, O Lord, the God of our fathers, creator of the changes of day and night, giving rest to the weary, renewing the strength of those who are spent, bestowing upon us occasions of song in the evening. As you have protected us in the day that is past, so be with us in the coming night; keep us from every sin, every evil, and every fear; for you are our light and salvation, and the strength of our life. To you be glory for endless ages. *Amen.*

A Litany of Intercession in the Night

O God Our Father, for the sake of the infinite love that burned in the heart of thy Son as he bore his passion, we plead for all tonight who stand most in need of thy merciful love and protection.

Try my heart, *as you visit me by night.*
For the wrongs we have committed and the good we have left undone, *have mercy.*
For all false judgments and uncharitable thoughts toward others, *have mercy.*
For presumption on thy grace and arrogance towards others, *have mercy.*
By thy humility in washing the disciples' feet, *save us, Jesus.*
For those in darkness this night, *save us, Jesus.*

On souls beset by temptation, *have mercy.*
On those in deadly sin, *have mercy.*
On those given up to worldliness and forgetful of thee, *have mercy.*
On those who are in danger of losing thee forever, *have mercy.*

By thine agony, *save them, Jesus.*
Those who are tempting others,
convert to thy love.
On those carrying on wicked trades and profiting by sin, *have mercy.*
On those indulging in sinful and exploitive amusements, *have mercy.*
On all imperiling their souls by luxury and self-indulgence, *have mercy.*
On all acting in cruel and vicious disregard of others, *have mercy.*

By thy scourging, *save them, Jesus.*
Those who suffer from the wickedness of others, *protect and restore by thy love.*

On all without home and shelter this night, *have mercy.*
On refugees and those whose homes are destroyed in war, *have mercy.*
On children abandoned or disowned by their families, *have mercy.*
On all in mental anguish, *have mercy.*
On those caught in addiction and destructive habits, *have mercy.*

On the hungry, the cold, and the frightened,
have mercy.

By thy cross and passion, *save them, Jesus.*
Those who are out to rescue and protect,
strengthen by thy love.

For those who work through the night hours,
have mercy.
For the police and first responders in crisis,
have mercy.
For those in transportation, *have mercy.*
For journalists, *have mercy.*
For those who clean and repair buildings or
infrastructure, *have mercy.*
For doctors and nurses, *have mercy.*
For all whose work sustains our community,
have mercy.

By thy nights spent watching in prayer,
save them, Jesus.
Those who work or watch or weep this night,
sustain with thy presence.

To the sick and the suffering, and all in agony
of body or mind, *give comfort and peace.*

To parents watching with sleepless children, to caregivers tending the elderly, to all who stand and watch over others this night,
give patience and steadfastness.

For the sleepless and the lonely, *be near them.*
For those in anxiety or mental distress,
calm them.
For those who this night will suffer bereavement, *visit and sustain them.*
To those who will die this night,
give hope and in thy mercy receive their souls.

On those dying suddenly and unprepared,
have mercy.
On those dying without hope or faith,
have mercy.
On those dying alone, *have mercy.*
To the faithful departed, especially *N.*
and any for whom no one prays,
grant light and peace.

To us sinners, now and in the hour of our death, *grant pardon of sins, renewal of faith, quickening of love, and a reasonable and holy hope in thee.*

By thy holy death, *deliver us, Jesus.*
By thy glorious resurrection, *save us and bring us all to the joys of paradise.*
For those who have said no prayers and for whom no one has prayed, let us say:

Our Father… Amen.

For the Evening

Almighty, everlasting God, let our prayer in your sight be as incense, the lifting up of our hands as the evening sacrifice. Give us grace to behold you, present in your Word and Sacraments, and to recognize you in the lives of those around us. Stir up in us the flame of that love which burned in the heart of your Son as he bore his passion, and let it burn in us to eternal life and to the ages of ages. *Amen.*

For Holy Rest

May the Lord support us all the day long,
Till the shades lengthen and the evening comes,
and the busy world is hushed,
and the fever of life is over,
and our work is done.
Then in his mercy may he give us a safe lodging, and holy rest, and peace at the last. *Amen.*

–John Henry Newman (1801–1890)

For Sleep

God our Father, by whose mercy the world turns safely into darkness and returns again to light: we place in your hands our unfinished tasks, our unsolved problems, and our unfulfilled hopes, knowing that only what you bless will prosper. To your love and protection we commit each other and all those we love, knowing that you alone are our sure defender, through Jesus Christ our Lord. *Amen.*

A Prayer at Bedtime

Holy One,
as the day comes to a close,
we place ourselves into your care.
Receive our gratitude for what gave us
life today,
and hold gently what was hard.
Soothe tired bodies and restless minds,
and grant rest that is deep and renewing.
As we sleep,
remind us the world does not rest on
our vigilance,
that we are accompanied by a love
that does not grow weary.

Let us wake restored,
ready to begin again.
Amen.

– Melissa Rau, Diocese of Southwest Florida

✠

God, I give this day to you. I give you all that I could do and all that I could not do. I lay down my questions and my desires. I relinquish my resentments and my fears. Hold me in the womb of darkness, Lord; swaddle me in starlight; help me dream of what can yet be born. Abide with me this night, so that I may walk with you in the day to come.
Amen.

– Phil Hooper, Diocese of Southern Ohio

✠

Night is drawing nigh.
For all that has been – Thanks!
For all that shall be – Yes!
Amen.

– Dag Hammarskjöld (1905–1961)

Family Prayers

Help Me Remember

Dear God,
Please help me when I feel nervous
before a test
    to remember I am smart.
Please help me when I feel anxious
    to remember to breathe.
Please help me when I feel afraid
    to remember I am loved.
Help all of us to remember we are smart,
brave, and loved,
    when we feel nervous, anxious, or afraid.
Amen.

– Carrie Melton, Age 9
Diocese of the Rio Grande

A Quiet Moment

I still my soul and make it quiet,
like a child upon its mother's breast;
    my soul is quieted within me. *Amen.*

– Psalm 131:4

Thank You God

Thank you God for my food.
Please let all the kids in the world
    have food on their tables.
I pray for all the people in hospitals
and in the whole world
    to heal and to be blessed. *Amen.*

– Brodie Marie Memba, Age 7
Diocese of Pennsylvania

Before Meals

Father God, as we gather around this table to break bread, we thank you for the food we are about to receive for the nourishment of our bodies. Please bless the hands that prepared this meal and every member of our family. As we are ever mindful that there are many in our community who are hungry and without resources, we pray that you will open a way for them to obtain sustenance. May we walk each day in light and love, as Christ loved us, and in his name we pray, *Amen.*

– Karen J. Vaughn, Diocese of Pennsylvania

A Prayer Before Meals

Source of life, we give thanks for this food and for all that made it possible: the earth that grew it and the hands that brought it to this table. Bless this meal and those who share it. May it nourish our bodies and steady our spirits. Keep us grateful without complacency, mindful of those who hunger, and generous with what we've been given. *Amen.*

For Protection

Dear Jesus, as a hen covers her chicks with her wings to keep them safe, protect us this day under your wings, for your mercy's sake. *Amen.*

✠

Dear God, be good to me.
The sea is so wide and my boat is so small.
Amen.

For Helpers

In the spirit of Fred Rogers

Dear God, thank you for all the helpers:
they keep us safe,
they help us learn and improve,
they think about others,
they are kind,
and they say please and thank you.
Help us all to be helpers. *Amen.*

– Lucy Melton, Age 9
Diocese of the Rio Grande

For Help

Help me, O God,
to remember you today.
I know that you never forget me.
Father, please protect my body.
Jesus, please open my heart.
Spirit, please guide my feet.
May this day be blessed,
and may I be a blessing to others. *Amen.*

Go God

For life – Go God!
For family – Go God!
For air – Go God!
For fun – Go God!
For land – Go God!
For water – Go God!
For food – Go God!
For fire – Go God!
For everything – Go God!
Amen.

– Jonathan Vasquez, Age 10
Diocese of Southwest Florida

A Bedtime Prayer

Ah, dearest Jesus, holy Child,
Make thee a bed, soft, undefiled
Within my heart, that it may be
A quiet chamber kept for thee.
Amen.

– Martin Luther (1483–1546)

God's Guidance

Inspired by Psalm 23

Lord, you are my shepherd;
I have everything I need.
You give me peace and guide me to do right.
Even when bad things happen,
I will not be afraid,
because you are there beside me.
Thank you for all you give me.
Lord, open my eyes to the truth of your Word.
Give me the wisdom to understand that I
will only get to greener pastures and
still waters if I totally submit to your
guidance.
Cause me to live in the world with my heart
and mind firmly anchored in heaven.
This I pray in Jesus' name, *Amen.*

– Nereya Rose Okeno, Diocese of Butere
Anglican Church of Kenya

For Grown-Ups

God of wonder,
somewhere along the way
we learned to take ourselves very seriously.

Invite us back to delight,
to curiosity that needs no answers,
to joy that surprises us
and opens us to life.

Free us from believing
that faith must always be heavy to be real,
or that responsibility leaves no room for play.

Give us permission to laugh at ourselves
and to follow what brings life.

Teach us again the wisdom of children:
how to trust,
how to imagine,
how to live fully,
in the moment before us.

Let our joy be holy,
our wonder be worship,
and our lives shaped by delight. *Amen.*

– Melissa Rau, Diocese of Southwest Florida

Keep Looking

Where is God?
In heaven!

Where is God?
In your heart!

Where is God?
In church!

Where is God?
Outside!

Where is God?
Keep looking.
Look in unexpected places.
Look in all the nooks and crannies.
Keep looking … you will find God.
Amen.

– Prekindergarten Class
Good Shepherd Preschool
Diocese of Southwest Florida

Personal Prayers

For God Within

Lord, revive your church, beginning with me. *Amen.*

✠

I find thee enthroned in my heart, my Lord Jesus. It is enough. I know that thou art throned in heaven. My heart and heaven are one. *Amen.*

–Alistair MacLean (1922–1987)

from The Breastplate of St. Patrick

Christ be with me, Christ within me,
Christ behind me, Christ before me,
Christ beside me, Christ to win me,
Christ to comfort and restore me.
Christ beneath me, Christ above me,
Christ in quiet, Christ in danger,
Christ in hearts of all that love me,
Christ in mouth of friend and stranger.
Amen.

Anima Christi

Soul of Christ, be my sanctification;
Body of Christ, be my salvation;
Blood of Christ, fill all my veins;
Water of Christ's side, wash out my stains;
Passion of Christ, my comfort be;
O good Jesus, listen to me;
In Thy wounds I fain would hide;
Ne'er to be parted from Thy side;
Guard me, should the foe assail me;
Call me when my life shall fail me;
Bid me come to Thee above,
With Thy saints to sing Thy love,
World without end.
Amen.

A Prophet's Prayer

Here I am! Send me.
Amen.

– Isaiah 6:8

Thou

Wherever I go, only Thou!
Wherever I stand, only Thou
Just Thou, again Thou!
Always Thou!
Thou, Thou, Thou!
When things are good, Thou!
When things are bad, Thou!
Thou, Thou, Thou!
Amen.

For God's Presence

God be in my head,
And in my understanding;
God be in my eyes
And in my looking;
God be in my mouth
And in my speaking;
God be in my heart
And in my thinking;
God be at my end,
And at my departing.
Amen.

For Help

O Lord Jesus, my Captain and my King,
Help my mind to think of you;
Help my eyes to look for you;
Help my lips to speak of you;
Help my hands to work for you;
Help my heart to love you,
All through the day. *Amen.*

– Bokang Maffa, Diocese of Pretoria
Anglican Church of Southern Africa

For Revelation

Dear God,
Please reveal to us your sublime beauty
that is everywhere, everywhere, everywhere,
so that we will never again feel frightened.
My divine love, my love,
please let us touch
your face.
Amen.

– Francis of Assisi (ca. 1181-1226)

For Less

Give us less, O Lord.

Give us fewer worries,
that we may come to you clear-headed.

Give us fewer angry moments,
that our relationships may be healed.

Give us less sorrow,
that we may have happy hearts.

Give us less doubt,
that our faith may remain strong.

Give us fewer obligations,
that there may be time enough.

Give us less, O Lord, of earth's mundane
things, that our path to you may not
waiver.

Give us less, O Lord. *Amen.*

– Sherri Killam-Albee
Diocese of the Central Gulf Coast

For Gifts of Love

O God,
Amidst the many dreads and distractions;
Among the cries of violence and vitriol;
Against the tide of worry and weary;
Perfect in us the gifts of your Love:
Of faith, increase it,
Of compassion, multiply it,
Of courage, strengthen it,
Of hope, establish it,
Of peace, ground it,
Of joy, kindle it,
Of truth, expand it.
For the sake of your grace and glory. *Amen.*

– Deon Johnson, Diocese of Missouri

For Understanding

Gracious and holy Father,
grant us the intellect to understand you,
reason to discern you, diligence to seek you,
wisdom to find you, a spirit to know you,
a heart to meditate upon you.

May our ears hear you,
may our eyes behold you,
and may our tongues proclaim you.
Give us grace that our way of life
may be pleasing to you,
that we may have the patience to wait for you
and the perseverance to look for you.
Grant us a perfect end—your holy presence,
a blessed resurrection and life everlasting.
We ask this through Jesus Christ our Lord.
Amen.

– Benedict of Nursia (ca. 480-547)

✠

Grant me, O Lord my God,
a mind to know you,
a heart to seek you,
wisdom to find you,
conduct pleasing to you,
faithful perseverance in waiting for you,
and a hope of finally embracing you.
Amen.

– Thomas Aquinas (1225–1274)

For All Goodness

Grant, O God, your protection;
and in your protection, strength;
and in strength, understanding;
and in understanding, knowledge;
and in knowledge, the knowledge of justice;
and in the knowledge of justice, the love of it;
and in that love, the love of existence;
and in the love of all existence,
the love of God,
God and all goodness. *Amen.*

Oblation

Take my heart! for I cannot give it Thee:
Keep it! for I cannot keep it for Thee.
Amen.

– Augustine of Hippo (354–430)

For Self-Mastery

O Lord, help us to master ourselves, that we may serve others. *Amen.*

For a Grateful Heart

Thou that hast giv'n so much to me,
Give one thing more, a grateful heart.
Amen.

– George Herbert (1593–1633)

For Discernment

I felt you stirring the other day.
I sensed that you have something to say,
That you are guiding my heart.
It is hard to wait for the fullness of time,
for completion.
In the meantime, I am thankful for the
listening, the yearning, the movement.
It tells me that you are making your way into
my being, my days, my life.
I felt you stirring the other day.
Now, with Mary, I say, "Let it be to me
according to your will." *Amen.*

– Marna Franson, Diocese of Northern Michigan

To Desire God

O Lord our God, grant us grace to desire Thee with our whole heart; that, so desiring, we may seek, and seeking find Thee; and so finding Thee may love Thee; and in loving Thee, may hate those sins from which Thou hast redeemed us, for the sake of Jesus Christ. *Amen.*

– Anselm of Canterbury (ca. 1033-1109)

To See God

Grant me to recognize in others, Lord God, the radiance of your own face. *Amen.*

– Pierre Teilhard de Chardin (1881–1955)

✠

Lord, lift thou up the light of thy countenance upon me, that in thy light I may see light: The light of thy grace today, and the light of thy glory hereafter. *Amen.*

– Lancelot Andrews (1555–1626)

For Healing Prejudice

Gracious God,
help us to regard all persons
as made in your image.
Create in us brave hearts
to acknowledge and address our prejudices.
Forgive the way we collude with silence
and imprison others in it.
Give us courage to speak words
that liberate and heal,
through Jesus Christ our Lord.
Amen.

✠

The things, good Lord, that we pray for, give us the grace to labor for. *Amen.*

– *Thomas More (1478–1535)*

For Commitment to Justice

God of justice and compassion
let us commit ourselves to bear the light of
the hope of our lives.
By the power of your Spirit,
you call us to be of one heart and mind
and to the work of lament and action.
From you comes power to give to others
the care we have ourselves received
so that we, and all who love your world,
may live in harmony and trust,
through Jesus Christ our Lord.
Amen.

A Prayer of Surrender

Into your hands I commend my spirit,
for you have redeemed me,
O LORD, O God of truth. *Amen.*

– Psalm 31:5

For Faith

I believe; help my unbelief! *Amen.*

– *Mark 9:24*

For Risk

Loving God, I don't know what to do next, how to move beyond the safety of habit and smallness. I want to be a good neighbor, as you call me to, but it seems so dangerous to move toward the margins, and sometimes I don't believe I would be welcome there, anyway. Help me find the strength to aim my life and witness past my discomfort and defensiveness. I want to risk being in relationships so deep that my responsibility to love and respect all of your creation outweighs my fear of failure. Give me the courage to care. *Amen.*

– *Maleah Rios, Diocese of California*

To See God in All

Compassionate God,
who sent Jesus Christ
to deliver us from all manner of injustices
and inequalities,
create in us new hearts and enlarged visions,
to see the image of God in every person
irrespective of background, race and
ethnicity.
May we be generous in our love of others
as we work towards ending
misunderstanding, racism and injustice;
creating communities of human flourishing,
through Jesus Christ your Son our Lord,
who is alive and reigns with you,
in the unity of the Holy Spirit,
one God, now and for ever.
Amen.

For Purpose

O Lord, let us not live to be useless. *Amen.*

– John Wesley (1703–1791)

A Confession

O most merciful Father; We confess before Thee that we have done little to spread Thy Gospel, and to extend Thy Kingdom among the people who know not Thee. Our love for the perishing world has been cold; our prayers have been feeble, and our gifts unworthy. We have not loved Thee as we ought, or our neighbor as ourselves. Hear us, O Lord, and when Thou hearest, forgive. Cast us not from Thy service, but of Thy mercy pardon all that is past, and quicken us by the Holy Spirit to living faith and burning zeal, through Jesus Christ our Lord. *Amen.*

For Guidance

O blessed Christ who didst draw near to the disciples as they walked together by the way and were sad, so draw near to us as we journey along our daily way. Open to us the meaning of life and reveal thyself as our strength and our companion as thou art our Lord and Savior evermore. *Amen.*

Turn Me Into Love

Lord do thou turn me all into love, and all my love into obedience, and let my obedience be without interruption, and there I hope thou wilt accept such a return as I can make.

Make me to be something that thou delightest in, and thou shalt have all that I am or have from thee, even whatsoever thou makest fit for thyself.

Teach me to live wholly for my Savior Jesus, and to be ready to die for Jesus, and to be conformable to his life and sufferings, and to be united to him by inseparable unions, and to own no passions but what may be servants to Jesus and disciples of his institution.

O sweetest Saviour, clothe my soul with thy holy robe; hide my sins in thy wounds, and bury them in thy grave; and let me rise in the life of grace, and abide and grow in it, till I arrive at the kingdom of glory. *Amen.*

– Jeremy Taylor (1613–1667)

For Light

Come, my Light, and illumine my darkness.
Come, my Life, and revive me from death.
Come, my Physician, and heal my wounds.
Come, Flame of divine love,
    and burn up the thorns of my sins,
kindling my heart with
    the flame of your love.
Come, my King, sit upon the throne of my
    heart and reign there.
For you alone are my King and my Lord.
Amen.

– Dmitri of Rostov (1651-1709)

For Healing

Heal me, O Lord, and I shall be healed; save me, and I shall be saved; for you are my praise. *Amen.*

– Jeremiah 17:14

To Live Like Jesus

Loving God,
teach us to love you,
teach us to love each other.
Generous God,
teach us to see you in the poor,
teach us to give with all our heart.
Compassionate God,
teach us to have mercy on those most
in need,
teach us to stand with those who are
broken and helpless.
Righteous God,
teach us to live like Jesus,
teach us to live lives directed towards all that
is good, true, and beautiful. *Amen.*

– Mark Francisco Bozzuti-Jones
Diocese of New York

✠

Take my life, and let it be
consecrated, Lord, to thee. *Amen.*

– Frances Ridley Havergal (1836-1879)

✠

Lord, take my lips and speak through them; take my mind and think through it; take my heart and set it on fire. *Amen.*

– W. H. H. Aitken (1841–1927)

For God's Will

Grant me, O Lord, to know
what I ought to know,
To love what I ought to love,
To praise what delights thee most,
To value what is precious in thy sight,
To hate what is offensive to thee.
Do not suffer me to judge according to the
sight of my eyes,
Nor to pass sentence according to the hearing
of the ears of ignorant men;
But to discern with a true judgment between
things visible and spiritual,
And above all, always to inquire what is the
good pleasure of thy will. *Amen.*

– Thomas à Kempis (ca. 1380–1471)

For Those Who Feel the Weight of Responsibility

Holy God, source of all wisdom and
  discernment:
Send your Spirit to guide and uphold me
  in my role of responsibility for others,
and in the choices I must make on their behalf.
Steer me away from overeager haste
  and undue delay,
and towards truthful and reliable information.
Help me digest what I need to know,
  and navigate complex systems.
Place gifted counsellors and friends in my path,
  and help me to listen well.
Give me your grace to face challenges
  and to think creatively under pressure.
Inspire my words with clarity and hope.
Renew me when I am fatigued,
  and remind me
with each question, decision, and task,
that all you desire is my faithful turning
  towards you day by day. *Amen.*

– Regina Walton, Diocese of Massachusetts

For a Servant's Heart

Thou who art over us,
Thou who art one of us,
Thou who art —
Also within us,
May all see Thee—in me also,
May I prepare the way for Thee,
May I thank Thee for all that
shall fall to my lot,
May I also not forget the needs of others,
Keep me in Thy love
As Thou wouldest that all should be
kept in mine.
May everything in this my being be directed
to Thy glory
And may I never despair.
For I am under Thy hand,
And in Thee is all power and goodness.

Give me a pure heart—that I may see Thee,
A humble heart—that I may hear Thee,
A heart of love—that I may serve Thee,
A heart of faith—that I may abide in Thee.
Amen.

– Dag Hammarskjöld (1905–1961)

For Truth

From the cowardice that dare not face
new truth,
From the laziness that is content with
half truth,
From the arrogance that thinks it knows
all truth:
Good Lord, deliver me!
Amen.

For Union with God

Eternal Light, shine into our hearts.
Eternal Goodness, deliver us from evil.
Eternal Power, be our support.
Eternal Wisdom, scatter the darkness
of our ignorance.
Eternal Pity, have mercy upon us.
That with all our heart and mind and soul
and strength we may seek thy face
and be brought by thine infinite mercy to thy
holy presence; through Jesus Christ our
Lord. *Amen.*

– Alcuin of York (ca. 732–804)

For Safety

Blessed are all Thy saints, my God and King, who have travelled over the tempestuous sea of mortality, and have at last made the desired port of peace and felicity. Oh, cast a gracious eye upon us who are still in our dangerous voyage. Remember and succor us in our distress, and think on them that lie exposed to the rough storms of troubles and temptations. Strengthen our weakness, that we may do valiantly in this spiritual war; help us against our own negligence and cowardice, and defend us from the treachery of our unfaithful hearts. We are exceeding frail, and indisposed to every virtuous and gallant undertaking. Grant, O Lord, that we may bring our vessel safe to shore, unto our desired haven. *Amen.*

– Augustine of Hippo (354–430)

For Grace

O Lord, who has taught us that to gain the whole world and to lose our souls is great folly, grant us the grace so to lose ourselves that we may truly find ourselves anew in the life of grace, and so to forget ourselves that we may be remembered in your kingdom. *Amen.*

– Reinhold Niebuhr (1892–1971)

For the Holy Spirit

Breathe in me, O Holy Spirit,
  That my thoughts may all be holy.
Act in me, O Holy Spirit,
  That my work, too, may be holy.
Draw my heart, O Holy Spirit,
  That I love but what is holy.
Strengthen me, O Holy Spirit,
  To defend all that is holy.
Guard me, then, O Holy Spirit,
  That I always may be holy. *Amen.*

– Augustine of Hippo (354–430)

✠

Spirit of the Living God,
  fall afresh on me,
Spirit of the Living God,
  fall afresh on me.
Break me, melt me,
  mold me, fill me.
Spirit of the Living God,
  fall afresh on me. *Amen.*

– Daniel Iverson (1890-1977)

Litanies

Litany of Thanksgiving

Let us give thanks to God our Father for all God's gifts so freely bestowed upon us.

For the beauty and wonder of your creation, in earth and sky and sea.

We thank you, Lord.

For all that is gracious in the lives of men and women, revealing the image of Christ,

We thank you, Lord.

For our daily food and drink, our homes and families, and our friends,

We thank you, Lord.

For minds to think, and hearts to love, and hands to serve,

We thank you, Lord.

For health and strength to work, and leisure to rest and play,

We thank you, Lord.

For the brave and courageous, who are patient in suffering and faithful in adversity,

We thank you, Lord.

For all valiant seekers after truth, liberty, and justice,

We thank you, Lord.

For the communion of saints, in all times and places,

We thank you, Lord.

Above all, we give you thanks for the great mercies and promises given to us in Christ Jesus our Lord; *To him be praise and glory, with you, O Father, and the Holy Spirit, now and forever. Amen.*

A Litany of Thanks

We are thankful for speech,
For access to words,
For our bodies seeking health, for our spirits seeking to be awakened.
Thank you, God.

We are thankful for the people put into our lives as teachers,
Even the frustrating ones,
Even the ones to whom we are related.
Thank you, God.

We are thankful for periwinkle skies and woolly clouds,
For grey days and tempestuous storms,
For the rustle of grass and the steadiness of rocky pathways.
Thank you, God.

We are thankful for our kids and others' kids,
And for once being a kid,
And for the promise of new beginnings embedded in kids' energetic bodies.
Thank you, God.

We are thankful for work,
    be it meaningful or mundane,
And for learning,
    both profound and profane.
Thank you, God.

We are thankful for community
That rubs up against us
    and makes us shiny, like polished stone,
For community that is the container,
For life's elements and moments,
For friends who calm us down and rile us up,
Who hold our hands or help us walk alone.
Thank you, God.

We are thankful for this day.
No, for this moment.
No, for this breath.
For eyes inclined to see
    the mere hint of a miracle,
For ears that listen to
    the harmony of the stars,
For laughter that celebrates
    humanity's foibles.
Thank you, God.

We are thankful for abundance
beyond our wildest dreams,
For not averting our gaze from those in pain,
For the desire to get out of bed
in the morning,
And for the blessed restoration of sleep.
Thank you, God.

For this life, in whatever form it takes.
We thank you, God. Amen.

– Marna Franson, Diocese of Northern Michigan

Litany for a Christian Home

Dear Father in Heaven, we name our family after Christ, Thy Son. And for our dwelling, our food, our health, for all who serve our home,

We thank Thee.

For making us dear to one another, for good times in happy union, and for all our many blessings,

We thank Thee.

That Thou wilt lead us day by day in ways of love and tenderness one to another,

We pray, Lord Jesus.

That each may stay close to all the rest; That we may be mindful one of another, with sympathy and understanding,

We pray, Lord Jesus.

That honest and cheerful, brave and true, we may be quick and ready to help each other meet the days' work and cares,

We pray, Lord Jesus.

That we may respect each others' rights and things, and that quarrels shall have no place in our tranquil home,

We pray, Lord Jesus.

For home life and its memories; for His keeping us one and secure; for Him in whom we live and trust,

Bless we our God.

For His whole Church in all the world, God's greater family, that bids us share Her gifts with God's children everywhere,

Bless we our God,
Father, Son, and Holy Spirit. Amen.

Litany for the Whole Church

God, you have begun a new creation in the Body of your Son. You have united matter with your Spirit and time with your eternity. We call this mystery *the Church*; it is the collision of grace and finitude; the crossroads of now and always. It is you and it is us, never parted again.

And so, with voices full of wonder, love, and praise, as the stewards and priests of your creation, we lift our voices as one, seeking *revelation*, *transformation*, and *action* as we become all that you have made us to be through Jesus Christ, our Lord.

We ask for your revelation:

That we may find our home in you as Father, Creator, and Source,

God, reveal it to us.

That we may know you in the world as Son, Word, and Wisdom,

God, reveal it to us.

That we may experience your Spirit's presence as Freedom, Inspiration, and Comfort,

God, reveal it to us.

That we may discover you in the faces of our neighbors and friends; of strangers and outcasts; of those we love and those we fear,

God, reveal it to us.

That we may understand your whole creation as good and worthy of care: the earth and its many life forms; the land, the seas, and the skies; the vast depths of the cosmos we cannot touch or see,

God, reveal it to us.

We ask for your transformation:

Through the reclamation of our original purpose as the caretakers of creation and the keepers of our brothers, sisters, and siblings,

God, transform us.

Through an abiding trust in your liberation of the forgotten, the lost, and those who travel through wilderness places,

God, transform us.

Through the acceptance of your prophetic call to do justice, love mercy, and walk humbly, whatever the cost,

God, transform us.

Through our surrender to the life, death, and resurrection of Jesus Christ, the one who stands astride heaven and earth,

God, transform us.

Through our participation in the communion of saints, in the unending worship of the heavenly chorus, and in the life that is beyond all death,

God, transform us.

We ask for the grace to act in covenant with you:

To continue in the teaching and fellowship of our ancestors in faith; in the reception of your Body and Blood; and in speaking the deepest prayers of our hearts,

God, embolden us.

To name what is evil and to resist it; to repent; to return to you; and to invite others to do the same,

God, embolden us.

To proclaim, by word and example, the Good News of your unconditional love for all people and for all of creation,

God, embolden us.

To seek and serve Christ in all persons, loving the stranger; the neighbor; the ones we call enemy; and even to love the reflection staring back from the mirror,

God, embolden us.

To strive for justice and peace among the whole earth; to respect the dignity of every creature; and to be the repairers of every breach between what is and what could be,

God, embolden us.

Lord have mercy.
Christ have mercy.
Lord have mercy.

In your mercy, *reveal* yourself to us, *transform* us, and *embolden* us, Lord, for the sake of your Kingdom. For you are the potter and we are your clay. You are the gardener and we are your soil. You are the author and we the unfurling scroll. Render from us something humble and whole; write upon our hearts something beautiful and true, and call us what you will.

Call us what we can be:

Call us blessed. *Call us blessed.*
Call us saved. *Call us saved.*
Call us redeemed. *Call us redeemed.*
Call us alive. *Call us alive.*
Call us found. *Call us found.*
Call us home. *Call us home.*
Call us beloved. *Call us beloved.*
Call us your own. *Call us your own.*
Call us the Church. *Call us the Church.*
And whatever we are called, let everyone and everything be called towards you, that we may step into the open door of your heart.

For this we pray and for this we live, through all things, above all things, and beyond all things, in the power of your most Holy Name. *Amen.*

– Phil Hooper, Diocese of Southern Ohio

A Litany Based on the Great "O Antiphons"

O WISDOM, proceeding from the Most High, reaching from one end to another, mightly and sweetly ordering all things: *Come and teach us the way of understanding.*

O ADONAI AND LEADER OF THE HOUSE OF ISRAEL, who appeared to Moses in the burning bush and on Mount Sinai gave the Law: *Come to deliver us with your strong arm.*

O ROOT OF JESSE, given as a sign for all peoples, in whose presence kings are silenced and before whom all nations will be judged: *Come with the day of peace and do not delay.*

O KEY OF DAVID, who opens and none can shut, leading us to life everlasting: *Come and lead out those bound in chains.*

O DAY SPRING, the bright and morning star, the eternal light that enlightens all: *Come and shine on those who sit in darkness and the shadow of death.*

O King of the Nations, chosen and precious cornerstone, binding in one all peoples: *Come quiet the strife that afflicts your children.*

O Emmanuel, the promise and the fulfillment of all promises: *Come and bring among us the joy of your kingdom.*

Even so, Lord Jesus, quickly come. *Amen.*

A New O Antiphons Litany

I

In the beginning God created….

O, Creatrix, from whose womb life is eternally becoming, ever new, ever intimate, quicken in us such immanent connection with you as yet-un-thought-of bud-burst-longing sees with songs' whispers wet with desert dew. Us re-blood.

Come, O holy floodwaters,
and transform the earth.

II

…and I shall dwell in the house
of the Lord for ever.

O Doma Vera, there is no nest, no cave, no cabin where we can be as fully ourselves as when we are at home with you. Help us to walk through the door of your presence every day of our lives.

Come, O holy habitation,
and be our only north, south, east, and west.

III

…and it was good.

O, Caritas, who loves every thing that you have made and weeps at the loss of a sparrow, create in us such hearts of flesh that we may love each other as you love us.

Come, O inexplicable giver,
and show us how it's done.

IV

…I am the Lord, your healer.

O, Salutifix, whose being is the wholeness that we long for, make of us, the dust of the stars and the dust of the earth, holy mud that we may apply ourselves to the wounds of our neighbors.

Come, O our health,
and make all manner of thing well.

V

…and I will take you for my people,
and I will be your God.

O, Fidelissima, through every end and every

beginning, enfold us in the peace of your always.

Come, O faithful companion,
and be our journey.

VI

All the ends of the earth…
shall turn to the Lord.

O, Eucharistia Gentium, every bird, every beast, every blade of grass feasts at the table of your open arms. And there are always enough chairs.

Come, O host of life, you are the banquet
where even enemies meet merrily.

VII

Arise…and come away…
for the winter is past….

O, Gaudium Nostrum, whose cosmic laughter makes the stars burn and our hearts burn and our minds leap in delight at discovering you everywhere, surprise us anew.

Come, O our joy.
Entwine us in your dancing. Amen.

– Carole-Jean Smith, Diocese of Massachusetts

A Beatitudes Litany

We remember, Lord Jesus, all who doubt and all who have been betrayed by those in power, that through the experience of your love they may learn to trust again.

Blessed are the poor in spirit
For theirs is the kingdom of heaven.

We remember, Lord Jesus, those who have died and all who are grieving, that through their loss they may come to know a larger wholeness (*especially...*).

Blessed are those who mourn
For they will be comforted.

We remember, Lord Jesus, those who are disregarded and forgotten: pour out your Spirit upon them that all may recognize their dignity and power.

Blessed are the meek
For they will inherit the earth.

We remember, Lord Jesus, all who struggle for freedom and justice; may the bread we break and the cup we share be tokens of our

solidarity with them and a sign of hope.
Blessed are those who hunger and thirst for righteousness
For they will be filled.

We remember, Lord Jesus, all who offer compassionate service to those who suffer, that through them your mercy may extended to all in need or trouble (*especially...*).
Blessed are the merciful
For they will receive mercy.

We remember, Lord Jesus, with gratitude all who seek the truth of your way of life: may their vision inspire us to live with awareness and renounce deception and distraction.
Blessed are the pure in heart
For they will see God.

We remember, Lord Jesus, your witness to the power of sacrificial love; may we share in your mission of reconciliation through the practice of nonviolent resistance to evil.
Blessed are the peacemakers
For they will be called children of God.

We remember, Lord Jesus, the prophets and apostles, martyrs and mystics, who have shone with the light of your love in dark times; may we be the light of the world in our day.

Blessed are those who are persecuted for righteousness' sake
For theirs is the kingdom of heaven.

We claim these promised blessings
in the strong name of Jesus.
Amen.

–John Kirkley, Diocese of California

Litany of the Holy Spirit

God the Father, source of all life,
have mercy upon us.
God the Son, by whom all things were made,
have mercy upon us.
God the Holy Spirit, the Lord
and giver of life, *have mercy upon us.*
Come Holy Spirit, fill the hearts of thy people,
and kindle in them the fire of thy love.

Promise of the Father,
Come, Holy Spirit.
Gift of the most high God,
Come, Holy Spirit.
Ray of heavenly light,
Come, Holy Spirit.
Author of all good,
Come, Holy Spirit.
Enduring love,
Come, Holy Spirit.

Spirit of truth and power,
fill the hearts of thy people.
Spirit of wisdom and understanding,
fill the hearts of thy people.
Spirit of counsel and might,
fill the hearts of thy people.
Spirit of knowledge and piety,
fill the hearts of thy people.
Spirit of the fear of the Lord,
fill the hearts of thy people.
Spirit of contrition and repentance,
fill the hearts of thy people.
Spirit of grace and prayer,
fill the hearts of thy people.

Spirit of love, joy, and peace,
fill the hearts of thy people.
Spirit of patience and gentleness,
fill the hearts of thy people.
Spirit of mildness and faith,
fill the hearts of thy people.
Spirit of purity and self-control,
fill the hearts of thy people.
Spirit of courage and conviction,
fill the hearts of thy people.
Spirit of adoption, giving confidence to the children of God, *fill the hearts of thy people.*

Spirit, moving on the face of the waters,
Come, Holy Spirit.
Spirit, speaking through the prophets,
Come, Holy Spirit.
Spirit, delighting in wisdom,
Come, Holy Spirit.
Spirit, overshadowing the Blessed Virgin Mary,
Come, Holy Spirit.
Spirit, poured out on Jesus at the Jordan,
Come, Holy Spirit.
Spirit, seen in tongues of fire on Pentecost,
Come, Holy Spirit.

Spirit, inspiring the Church's witness,
Come, Holy Spirit.
Spirit, still leading the Church into truth,
Come, Holy Spirit.
Spirit, filling all the world,
Come, Holy Spirit.

Come, Holy Spirit, and renew the face of the earth, *fill the hearts of thy people.*
Shed light of understanding and wisdom,
fill the hearts of thy people.
To make us obedient to thy leading,
fill the hearts of thy people.
To quicken our love and broaden our compassion, *fill the hearts of thy people.*
To teach us to pray and enliven our worship,
fill the hearts of thy people.
To give us perseverance and courage,
fill the hearts of thy people.
Come, Holy Spirit,
Fill the hearts of thy people,
and kindle in us the fire of thy love.
Create in us a clean heart, O God,
And renew a right spirit within us.

Grant, Gracious God, that thy Holy Spirit may enlighten and cleanse our hearts and that, through the abundance of the Spirit's gifts, we may be fruitful in all good works; through Jesus Christ our Lord. *Amen.*

The Litany of the Saints

Lord, have mercy upon us.
Christ, have mercy upon us.
Lord, have mercy upon us.

O Christ, hear us,
O Christ, graciously hear us.

God the Father of heaven,
    have mercy upon us.
God the Son, redeemer of the world,
    have mercy upon us.
God the Holy Spirit, sanctifier of the faithful,
    have mercy upon us.

Holy Mary Mother of God, *pray for us.*
Saint Michael, *pray for us.*

Saint Gabriel, *pray for us.*
Saint Raphael, *pray for us.*
All ye holy angels and archangels, *pray for us.*
All ye holy orders of blessed spirits, *pray for us.*
Saint John the Baptist, *pray for us.*
Saint Joseph, *pray for us.*

All ye holy patriarchs and prophets, *pray for us.*
Saint Peter, *pray for us.*
Saint Paul, *pray for us.*
Saint Andrew, *pray for us.*
Saint James, *pray for us.*
Saint John, *pray for us.*
Saint Thomas, *pray for us.*
Saint Philip, *pray for us.*
Saint Bartholomew, *pray for us.*
Saint Matthew, *pray for us.*
Saint Simon, *pray for us.*
Saint Thaddeus, *pray for us.*
Saint Matthias, *pray for us.*
Saint Barnabas, *pray for us.*
Saint Luke, *pray for us.*
Saint Mark, *pray for us.*

All ye holy apostles and evangelists, *pray for us.*
All ye holy disciples of the Lord, *pray for us.*
All ye holy innocents, *pray for us.*
Saint Stephen, *pray for us.*
Saint Lawrence, *pray for us.*
Saint Vincent, *pray for us.*
Saints Fabian and Sebastian, *pray for us.*
Saints John and Paul, *pray for us.*
Saints Cosmas and Damian, *pray for us.*
Saints Gervase and Protase, *pray for us.*

All ye holy martyrs, *pray for us.*
Saint Sylvester, *pray for us.*
Saint Gregory, *pray for us.*
Saint Ambrose, *pray for us.*
Saint Augustine of Hippo, *pray for us.*
Saint Jerome, *pray for us.*
Saint Martin, *pray for us.*
Saint Nicholas, *pray for us.*

All ye holy bishops and confessors, *pray for us.*
All ye holy doctors, *pray for us.*
Saint Anthony, *pray for us.*
Saint Benedict, *pray for us.*

Saint Bernard, *pray for us.*
Saint Dominic, *pray for us.*
Saint Francis, *pray for us.*

All ye holy priests and Levites, *pray for us.*
All ye holy monks and hermits, *pray for us.*
Saint Mary Magdalene, *pray for us.*
Saint Agatha, *pray for us.*
Saint Lucy, *pray for us.*
Saint Agnes, *pray for us.*
Saint Cecilia, *pray for us.*
Saint Catherine, *pray for us.*
Saint Anastasia, *pray for us.*
Saint Helena, *pray for us.*
All ye holy virgins and widows, *pray for us.*
All ye holy servants and handmaids of God,
make intercession for us.

Be favorable, *spare us, O Lord.*
Be favorable, *graciously hear us, O Lord.*
From all evil, *deliver us, O Lord.*
From all sin, *deliver us, O Lord.*
From thy wrath, *deliver us, O Lord.*

From a sudden and unprepared death,
deliver us, O Lord.
From the snares of the devil,
deliver us, O Lord.
From anger and hatred and all evil will,
deliver us, O Lord.
From pride and despair, *deliver us, O Lord.*
From presumption and coldness of heart,
deliver us, O Lord.
From all lack of charity and from any malicious thoughts, *deliver us, O Lord.*
From lightning and tempest,
deliver us, O Lord.
From earthquake, pestilence, and famine,
deliver us, O Lord.
From war, violence, and oppression,
deliver us, O Lord.
From everlasting death, *deliver us, O Lord.*

By the mystery of thy holy Incarnation,
deliver us, O Lord.
By thy Advent, *deliver us, O Lord.*
By thy Nativity, *deliver us, O Lord.*
By thy Baptism and holy fasting,
deliver us, O Lord.

By thy cross and passion, *deliver us, O Lord.*
By thy death and burial, *deliver us, O Lord.*
By thy holy Resurrection, *deliver us, O Lord.*
By thy glorious Ascension, *deliver us, O Lord.*
By the coming of the Holy Spirit, the comforter, *deliver us, O Lord.*
In the Day of Judgment, *deliver us, O Lord.*

We sinners do beseech thee to hear us, and that it may please thee to spare us,
We beseech thee to hear us, good Lord.
That it may please thee to pardon and forgive us, *We beseech thee to hear us, good Lord.*
That it may please thee to bring us to true repentance,
We beseech thee to hear us, good Lord.
That it may please thee to govern and preserve thy holy Church,
We beseech thee to hear us, good Lord.
That it may please thee to keep all bishops, priests, and deacons,
We beseech thee to hear us, good Lord.
That it may please thee to grant increase of faith, hope, and charity to all thy people,

We beseech thee to hear us, good Lord.

That those in authority may serve justice, pursue peace, and walk in righteousness,

We beseech thee to hear us, good Lord.

That it may please thee to preserve to our use the fruits of the earth,

We beseech thee to hear us, good Lord.

That all peoples may live in security and rejoice in thy bountiful creation,

We beseech thee to hear us, good Lord.

That it may please thee to strengthen and preserve us in thy service,

We beseech thee to hear us, good Lord.

That it may please thee to lift our minds to heavenly desires,

We beseech thee to hear us, good Lord.

That it may please thee to reward with eternal blessings all our benefactors,

We beseech thee to hear us, good Lord.

That it may please thee to deliver our souls and the souls of our kinfolks, friends, and benefactors from everlasting damnation,

We beseech thee to hear us, good Lord.

That it may please thee to grant to all faithful departed ✠ eternal rest and peace,
We beseech thee to hear us, good Lord.

Son of God, we beseech thee to hear us.
Son of God, we beseech thee to hear us.
O Lamb of God, that takest away the sins of the world, *spare us, O Lord.*
O Lamb of God, that takest away the sins of the world, *graciously hear us, O Lord.*
O Lamb of God, that takest away the sins of the world, *have mercy upon us.*
O Christ, hear us. *O Christ, hear us. Amen.*

The Litany of the Saints may end at this point, with the Lord's Prayer or a collect.

A Personal Litany

I pray to thank God for all the good things
in my life.
I pray for my loved ones.
I pray for the people I know.
I pray for the people I have met.
I pray for people I don't know.
I pray for those who are in need.
I pray that the comfort of the Spirit may
accompany everyone.
I pray that those who suffer may be helped.
I pray that those who are weary may
find rest.
I pray that those who ask for nothing,
may be kept close to God's heart.
For all I cannot express in words, I thank you, Lord;
with sighs too deep for words, I implore you, Lord.

I pray for the earth and nature.
I pray that we may respect them,
more each day.
I pray for those who work for the
environment.

I pray for those who work to feed us.
I pray for those who work with animals.
I pray for those who work to change our lifestyles for the better.
I pray for those who seek solutions.
I pray for those who try to persuade our leaders.
I pray for those who must make collective decisions.
I pray that we all move forward with more humility and sustainability.

For all I cannot express in words, I thank you, Lord;
with sighs too deep for words, I implore you, Lord.

I pray for those who are in distress.
I pray for those who are in pain.
I pray for those who are suffering.
I pray for those who are grieving.
I pray for those who are in darkness.
I pray that God will bring them comfort.
I pray that God will cover them with God's wings.
I pray that God will bring them solutions and support.

I pray that God will bring them peace.
I pray that God will hear their prayers.
For all I cannot express in words, I thank you, Lord;
with sighs too deep for words, I implore you, Lord.

I pray for those who are single.
I pray for those who are in love.
I pray for those who are pregnant.
I pray for those who have children.
I pray for those who desire all of this
but do not have it.
I pray for those who work.
I pray for those who are looking for a job.
I pray for those who are studying.
I pray for those who are searching for their path.
I pray for children.
For all I cannot express in words, I thank you, Lord;
with sighs too deep for words, I implore you, Lord.

I pray for those who care for others.
I pray for those who serve others.
I pray for those who are forgotten.
I pray for those who are discriminated
against.
I pray for those who are marginalized.

I pray for those who are deprived of their
freedoms.
I pray for those who have lost hope.
I pray that God will enlighten them
with revelation.
I pray that people of goodwill come to
their aid.
I pray that our hearts may be renewed and
opened to love and compassion.

For all I cannot express in words, I thank you, Lord;
with sighs too deep for words, I implore you, Lord.
Amen.

– Marie Bellando Bitjans
Convocation of Episcopal Churches in Europe

Invocations to Christ

O Son of Mary: *Consecrate our homes.*
Son of David: *Cleanse our politics.*
Son of Man: *Rule the affairs of Nations.*
Son of God: *Give us eternal life.*
Jesus the carpenter: *Hallow our daily work.*
Jesus the Christ: *Deliver a world which waits for thee.*
Jesus the Savior: *Save us from ourselves.*
Jesus the life-giver: *Renew thy Church.*
Word of God: *Perfect thy creation.*
Lord exalted at the Father's side: *Raise us to live with thee in God. Amen.*

Blessings

Blessings

May our Lord Jesus Christ
be near you to defend you,
within you to refresh you,
around you to preserve you,
before you to guide you,
behind you to justify you,
above you to bless you;
and the blessing of almighty God,
the Father, the Son, and the Holy Spirit,
be among you and remain with you always.
Amen.

✠

May the love of the Lord Jesus
draw us to himself;
May the power of the Lord Jesus
strengthen us in his service;
May the joy of the Lord Jesus
fill our souls.
Amen.

✠

O God, Author of eternal light, do Thou shed forth continual day upon us who watch for Thee; that our lips may praise Thee, our life may bless Thee, our meditations may glorify Thee; through Christ our Lord. *Amen.*

A Trinitarian Blessing

May God the Father bless us.
May God the Son heal us.
May God the Holy Spirit enlighten us,
and give us
eyes to see with,
ears to hear with,
hands to do the work of God with,
feet to walk with,
a mouth to preach the word of salvation with,
and the angel of peace to watch over us and lead us at last,
by our Lord's gift, to the Kingdom.
Amen.

– Dominic de Guzmán (1170–1221)

To Be a Blessing

Loving God,
bless our food,
    bless those who have no food.

Loving God,
bless our love,
    bless those who have no love.

Loving God,
bless our homes.
    bless refugees and immigrants everywhere,
    bless those who are unhoused
    and in prison.

Loving God,
bless us,
    that we might be blessings for others.
Amen.

– Mark Francisco Bozzuti-Jones
Diocese of New York

Gaelic Blessing

Deep peace of the running wave to you.
Deep peace of the flowing air to you.
Deep peace of the quiet earth to you.
Deep peace of the shining stars to you.
Deep peace of the Son of peace to you.
Amen.

A Blessing for All People

The blessings of the Lord rest and remain upon all His people in every land, of every tongue; the Lord meet in mercy all that seek Him; the Lord comfort all who suffer and mourn; the Lord hasten His coming, and give us, His people, the blessing of peace. *Amen.*

– Handley Carr Glyn Moule (1841–1920)

Beatitudes

Blessed are the poor in spirit,
for theirs is the kingdom of heaven.
Blessed are those who mourn,
for they will be comforted.
Blessed are the meek,
for they will inherit the earth.
Blessed are those who hunger and thirst for
righteousness, for they will be filled.
Blessed are the merciful,
for they will obtain mercy.
Blessed are the pure in heart,
for they will see God.
Blessed are the peacemakers,
for they will be called children of God.
Blessed are those who are persecuted for
righteousness' sake,
for theirs is the kingdom of heaven. *Amen*

– Matthew 5:3-10

A Blessing for You Who Reads This

The Lord bless you and keep you.
The Lord make his face to shine upon you
and be gracious to you.
The Lord lift up his countenance upon you
and give you peace. *Amen.*

Acknowledgments

This book is the expression of the many praying hearts and helping hands that have touched its making, partners both known and unknown, within and beyond Forward Movement.

We are grateful to all those editors at Forward Movement who, across a decade and a half, have helped to dream—and labor—this book into being.

We are grateful to our partners at the Episcopal Church's United Thank Offering, especially Heather Melton and Karin Elsen, who partnered with us to broaden the voices of prayer we hear here.

We are grateful to all the individual contributors who have shared their prayers with us or written new ones specifically for this volume:

Barbara Ballenger, Diocese of Pennsylvania

Marie Bellando Bitjans, Convocation of Episcopal Churches in Europe

Mark Francisco Bozzuti-Jones, Diocese of New York

Shaneequa Brokenleg, Diocese of South Dakota

Alice Briscoe Brown, Diocese of Pennsylvania

Andy Doyle, Diocese of Texas

Margaret Ellsworth, Diocese of Idaho

Barb Hagen, Diocese of Wisconsin

Caroline Hamilton-Arnold, Disciples of Christ, Houston, TX

Phil Hooper, Diocese of Southern Ohio

Kurt Huber, Cheyenne River Episcopal Mission, Diocese of South Dakota

Marna Franson, Diocese of Northern Michigan

Annie Kate Jacobs, Diocese of East Carolina

Deon Johnson, Diocese of Missouri

Sherri Killam-Albee, Diocese of the Central Gulf Coast

John Kirkley, Diocese of California

Kristin LeMay, Diocese of Southern Ohio

Kathy Lenox, Diocese of Western Oregon

Bokang Maffa, Diocese of Pretoria, Anglican Church of Southern Africa

Ruth Marston-Bihl, United Methodist Church, Seattle, WA

Cody Maynus, Diocese of Minnesota

Miriam McKenney, Diocese of Southern Ohio

Carrie Melton, Age 9, Diocese of the Rio Grande

Lucy Melton, Age 9, Diocese of the Rio Grande

Brodie Marie Memba, Age 7, Diocese of Pennsylvania

Cara Ellen Modisett, Diocese of Southwestern Virginia

Nereya Rose Okeno, Diocese of Butere, Anglican Church of Kenya

Prekindergarten Class, Good Shepherd Preschool, Diocese of Southwest Florida

Melissa Rau, Diocese of Southwest Florida

Carlos Respeito, Diocese of Lebombo, Anglican Church of Mozambique and Angola

Maleah Rios, Diocese of California

Carole-Jean Smith, Diocese of Massachusetts

Twila Smith, Diocese of Oklahoma

Noah Stansbury, Diocese of Texas

Kay Sylvester, Diocese of Los Angeles

Jonathan Vasquez, Age 10, Diocese of Southwest Florida, in memory of Jim Pazynski who always prayed, "Go God!"

Karen J. Vaughn, Diocese of Pennsylvania

Regina Walton, Diocese of Massachusetts

We give thanks to and for you all, for helping us to pray with and for one another in the rich diversity of our varied voices.

We are grateful, too, to our sister churches in the worldwide Anglican Communion—the Anglican Church of Canada, the Church of England, the Church of Nigeria, the Church of South India—whose prayer books and liturgical resources have broadened our prayer. We are thankful, as well, to pray together here with words from our cousins in the Christian Church (Disciples of Christ), the Evangelical Lutheran Church, the Presbyterian Church USA, and the United Methodist Church.

We offer this volume in gratitude and humility, hoping that these pages will deepen our practice, strengthen our faith, build up the church, and knit us together in love as we lift aloud the hopes, cares, and concerns of our many hearts. We join our voices to yours and to all the company of heaven past, present, and yet to come.

Pray for us, as we pray for you, in hope, and in the name of Jesus.

NOTES

Many of the prayers in this volume come from or were adapted from The Book of Common Prayer (1979) or Forward Movement's prayer collections, *Prayers New & Old*, *Prayers for All Occasions*, and *Saint Augustine's Prayer Book.*

Prayers were also drawn from the very earliest publications of Forward Movement: *Discipleship* (1935), *Follow On* (1935), and *Forward Day by Day* (beginning in 1935).

Select prayers are reprinted from the following sources:

Page 75: *Book of Alternative Services*, Anglican Church of Canada.

Pages 28, 47, 122: *Prayers of the Evangelical Lutheran Church in America.*

Pages 155, 187, 188, 190: The Church of England's "Liturgical Resources for Black History Month," 2021. Used by permission.

Page 155: *The Book of Common Worship*, Copyright © 2004 by The Church of South India. Reprinted with permission.

Page 36: *The Book of Common Prayer*. Copyright © 1996 by The Church of Nigeria.

Pages 12, 86 (adapted): *The Book of Occasional Services*. Copyright © 2023 by The Domestic and Foreign Missionary Society of the Protestant Episcopal Church. Reprinted with the permission of Church Publishing Incorporated.

Prayers not from these sources or otherwise noted are written by Forward Movement staff, past and present, were contributed by friends around the Church, or are in the public domain.

Permission has been granted to reprint the following selections:

Martha Blacklock, "The Prayer of Jesus." Used by permission of the author.

Dag Hammarskjöld, "Hallowed be Thy name,/ not mine...," "Before Thee, Father,...," "Night is drawing nigh...," and "Thou who art over us..." from *Markings*, translated by W. H. Auden and Leif Sjoberg. Copyright © 1963 by Albert Bonniers Förlag AB. Translation copyright © 1964 and renewed 1992 by Alfred A. Knopf, Inc. and Faber & Faber, Ltd. Used by permission of Alfred A. Knopf, an imprint of the Knopf Doubleday Publishing Group, a division of Penguin Random House LLC. All rights reserved.

Meister Eckhart, "Apprehend God in all things," from *Meditations with Meister Eckhar*t by Matthew Fox, published by Inner Traditions Intrnational and Bear & Company. Copyright © 1983 by Bear & Company, Inc. All rights reserved. Reprinted by permission of the publisher.

Hildegard of Bingen, "Holy Spirit, bestowing life unto life," translated by Norma Gentile. Reprinted with the permission of the translator.

INDEX

ABOUT US

At Forward Movement, our mission is to inspire disciples and empower evangelists. Best known for the daily devotional *Forward Day by Day*—available in print, podcast, app, and in Braille and Spanish (*Adelante día a día*)—we also offer books, small-group studies, apps, podcasts, video courses, online communities, and conferences, all aiming to reinvigorate the life of the church by turning habitual Christians into devoted followers of Jesus Christ.

A ministry of the Episcopal Church since 1935, Forward Movement is an independent nonprofit organization funded by the sale of our resources and by gifts from generous donors.

Explore our resources, support our ministry, and find inspiration for your own spiritual journey at **forwardmovement.org.**

Maranatha

Amen. Come, Lord Jesus.